The Decentring of the Traditional University

The Decentring of the Traditional University provides a unique perspective on the implications of media change for learning and literacy that allows us to peer into the future of (self) education. Each chapter draws on sociocultural and activity theory to investigate how resourceful students are breaking away from traditional modes of instruction and educating themselves through engagement with a globally interconnected web-based participatory culture.

The argument is developed with reference to the findings of an ethnographic study that focused on university students' informal uses of social and participatory media. Each chapter draws attention to the shifting locus of agency for regulating and managing learning and describes an emergent genre of learning activity. For example, Francis explores how students are cultivating and nurturing *globally distributed funds of living knowledge* that transcend institutional boundaries and describes students *learning through serious play in virtually figured worlds* that support radically personalised life-long learning agendas. Further, each chapter highlights the challenges and choices learners confront as they struggle to negotiate the fault lines of media convergence and master the new media literacies required to exploit the full potential of Web 2.0 as a learning resource.

Overall, this compelling argument proposes that we are witnessing a period of historic systemic change in the culture of university learning as an emergent web-based participatory culture starts to disrupt and displace a top-down culture industry model of education that has evolved around the medium of the book. As a result, Francis argues that we need to re-conceive higher education as an identity-project in which students work on their projective identities (or imagined future selves) through engagement with both formal and informal learning activities.

Russell Francis is Research Fellow at the Department of Education, University of Oxford, UK and a Postdoctoral Fellow at the Linneaus Centre for Research on Learning, Interaction and Mediated Communications in Contemporary Society (LinCS), University of Gothenburg, Sweden.

The Decentring of the Traditional University

The future of (self) education in virtually figured worlds

Russell Francis

Routledge
Taylor & Francis Group

LONDON AND NEW YORK

This edition published 2010
by Routledge
2 Park Square, Milton Park, Abingdon, Oxon OX14 4RN

Simultaneously published in the USA and Canada
by Routledge
270 Madison Avenue, New York, NY 10016

Routledge is an imprint of the Taylor & Francis Group, an informa business

© 2010 Russell Francis

Typeset in Garamond by Wearset Ltd, Boldon, Tyne and Wear
Printed and bound in Great Britain by TJI Digital, Padstow,
Cornwall

British Library Cataloguing in Publication Data
A catalogue record for this book is available from the British Library

Library of Congress Cataloging-in-Publication Data
A catalog record has been requested for this book

ISBN: 978-0-415-55053-6 (hbk)
ISBN: 978-0-203-85802-8 (ebk)

Contents

List of illustrations   viii
Preface by Anne Edwards   ix
Acknowledgements   xiv

Introduction   1

1 From the culture industry to participatory culture   8

*Understanding media change: from the culture industry to
    participatory culture 8*
Media change and learning 12
Peering into the future of (self) education 16
Research site, informants and data collection 18

2 Cognitive anthropology on the Cyberian frontier   22

Introduction 22
Sociocultural and activity theory: an overview 22
Cognitive anthropology and studies of cognition in the wild 31
*Expansive learning: double binds, breaking away and horizontal
    developments 32*
Projective identities and virtually figured worlds 35
Digitally mediated practice as new media literacy 37
Summary 40

3 The learner as designer   42

Introduction 42
Understanding the learner as designer 43
The scope of design work in the new media age 48
The challenges and choices confronting the learner as designer 50
Towards a theory of mindful design 52
Summary 55

4   **Creative appropriation, new media and
    self-education**   56

Introduction 56
The concept of creative appropriation expanded 57
Breaking away from the traditional university 58
Creative appropriation and authentic need 64
Creative appropriation: driving cultural change from the bottom up 66
Identity as a mediator and motivator of learning activity 67
Challenges, choices and new media literacies 71
Summary 74

5   **Globally distributed funds of living knowledge**   75

Introduction 75
*Conceptual building blocks for understanding collaborative learning
    beyond the networked university 77*
The formation of a fund of living knowledge 78
*Cultivating and nurturing globally distributed funds of living
    knowledge 81*
Mobilizing a globally distributed funds of living knowledge 85
Nurturing a globally distributed fund of living knowledge 88
Challenges, choices and new media literacies 89
Summary 92

6   **Learning through serious play in virtually figured
    worlds**   94

Bruner and the narrative construction of self 95
Learning by being in immersive game worlds 97
Worldmaking as self-making 98
Serious play, history in laptop and committed learning 102
Virtually figured worlds as expanded spaces of self-authoring 104
Lifelong learning beyond institutional boundaries 106
Summary 110

7   **The decentring of the traditional university**   112

Introduction 112
*Two approaches to understanding the implications of media
    change 112*
*Conceptualizing higher education with the aid of Engeström's
    extended mediational triangle 114*
Are we witnessing the decentring of the traditional university? 118

Implications for educational policy and practice 121
Directions for further research 123
Towards a developmental research agenda 128

Appendix: Data collection strategy and methods   130

Notes   135
Bibliography   138
Index   148

Illustrations

Figures

1.1 Proportionate use of Web 2.0 tools for socializing, study and
    work related activities   14
4.1 Screenshot of the 'Understanding ANOVA Visually' website   60
7.1 Higher education as self-making activity   115

Tables

1.1 Demographics of students recruited for the study   19
1.2 List of hobbies and interests involving the use of the Internet   20

Preface
Anne Edwards

One of the pleasures of doing social research is that just sometimes you find yourself riding the wave: picking up on changes and disturbances in the field you are studying that propel you forward fast into exciting areas of thinking, and allow you to see connections that would not have been visible to you unless you were willing to look ahead, keep focused on the field and enjoy the challenges. Together with John Furlong I was able to watch Russ ride the wave that arose out connecting the developing use of new media tools with accounts of students' experiences as learners in higher education. Russ kept his balance by first clinging fast to the concepts offered by sociocultural and activity theory views of learning and ultimately stretching those ideas to fit the phenomena he was observing.

One of the problems facing social researchers, and perhaps it is particularly true of old-stagers, is that we can become so trusting of the tools we use when digging away at society that our actions become restricted and we miss new features in the worlds we are examining. That is not the case here. Able to dwell in the phenomena over the period of doctoral and post-doctoral study, Russ has sharpened the analytic tools in his toolbox as he has dug. The outcome is a fascinating account of the interplay between the resources that support university students' learning and their experiences and identities as learners. At the same time the account is strengthened by making some freshly sharpened analytic tools available to us.

How Russ refined the tools is typically Vygotskian. Staying close to his data with detailed accounts of how students used media to support their learning he started by scraping away with established resources such as 'figured worlds' (Holland *et al.* 1998) and 'funds of knowledge' (Moll and Greenberg 1990). He then refashioned them in response to what he found in the field so that 'virtually figured worlds' became a central construct as did the idea of 'globally distributed funds of knowledge'. These are not brand new concepts, but are refinements made in lengthy iterations of concept and world, with a focus on trying to understand how university students learn with new media.

The learning practices of students in higher education are a good place to start an exploration of how new media may shape identities, activities and the potentially distributed practices of knowledge work. Higher education is a place where young scholars can try out ideas and possible selves and there we can perhaps discover more about how new media contribute to shaping the worlds in which we create our identities. Rückriem, for example, recently suggested that we should recognise that the idea of the knowledge society represents 'a radical new form of global socialization, which makes possible new forms of self-creation and self-definitions for individuals' (2009: 93). However, he continues: 'Most activity theorists are not aware of the importance of these transformation processes or at least do not assess them adequately' (ibid.). I suggest that this text is one attempt at tackling this gap. However, this is not a book *about* activity theory or sociocultural approaches to learning. Rather the ideas that are part of the Vygotskian legacy are used to help us understand emerging themes in a rapidly changing educational landscape and to point us towards some of the implications for universities in particular.

How useful have sociocultural and activity theory ideas been? The cultural shaping of mind is now a commonly understood feature of sociocultural theory and the role of cultural tools as mediating or mind-shaping devices is widely recognised. Here Bruner summarises these foundational features of the approach.

> Human functioning in a cultural setting, mental and overt, is shaped by the culture's toolkit of 'prosthetic devices'. We are a tool-using, tool-making species par excellence, and we rely on 'soft tools' as much as on digging sticks and stone-choppers – culturally devised ways of thinking, searching and planning.
>
> (Bruner 1996: 168)

As ever, Bruner weaves together ideas in ways which belie their complexity. Let us therefore unpack this statement. Human functioning clearly involves thinking as well as acting and both are shaped by culturally produced tools. But not only are we tool-using, we are also tool-making. We not only internalise what is culturally valued, we externalise our understandings and intentions and act on and therefore shape our worlds and the tools we use in them in ways that suit us and those whose values we share. Moreover, how we externalise and act on the world is shaped by the historical practices in which we find ourselves and which we in turn reshape as we work in them.

This constant dialectic between mind and world, mediated by the tools which we fashion and refashion as the world changes, is central to learning. However, the freedom of movement needed for the dialectic is perhaps more easily found 'in the wild' outside education than in most formal educational settings, where there are curricula to be followed and specific mediational means to be mastered in approved and accredited ways.

The students in the study at the centre of this book were postgraduates who, even on taught courses, are less trammelled by rigid curricula and assessment systems than are students in schools. The boundaries between the certainties of thinking and acting to be found in schools and the often more exploratory and tentative ways of working to be found in, for example, research are not evident at postgraduate level in most universities. Masters students therefore experience more freedom of movement and more opportunity to use tools, such as social software or online special interest groups, which support their identities and actions in the wild, when taking forward their intentions as students. Nonetheless the arguments in this book raise questions for the entire education system.

At first sight it makes complete sense for students to create personal learning environments which support their projective identities while they are relatively briefly following masters or doctoral studies. Online networked communities and the personal and collective capital that accrue there transcend the 'now' and 'here' aspects of the college world and potentially have a much longer life. There are also other advantages. Students come to their studies with expertise in navigating what *pace* Holland *et al.* (1998), Russ has described as the 'virtually figured worlds'. Let us stay a little longer with expertise, which I have described elsewhere (Edwards 2010) as including the capacity of 'working resourcefully with others' to take forward one's intentions.

The interplay between the figured worlds of specific practices such as being a student or an environmentalist and the actions that occur in activities within them, is central to a sociocultural explanation of how people become expert within practices. Holland and her colleagues (1998) have observed what they describe as a qualitative change between individuals and the practices they inhabit. It occurs when people move from being merely proficient in following the rules of a practice to being able to expertly devise their own moves and regulate their own actions within the practice. This change, Holland *et al.* suggest, means that individuals begin to understand themselves in terms of the activity in the cultural world. The intentional manipulation of features of practices is therefore also a matter of identity formation. This view, along with other culturally oriented explanations of expertise, see expertise and identity as integral to the successful accomplishment of activities in practices. Consequently self-regulation, and the intentional and agentic action that accompanies it, are important qualities to be developed among learners.

The expertise developed in practices in the online networked communities discussed in this book had over time shaped the personal learning environments that the students created. They could continue to work intentionally within them without feeling deskilled by a move from, for example, the practices of undergraduate study in California to those of postgraduate study in England. But there was more to it than that. Russ has drawn on Gee's (2003, 2004) powerful notion of projective identities to label how and why some students were able to engage in activities in ways which propelled them forward towards the future identities they were beginning to fashion.

Russ describes the students' shaping of projective identities such as 'the policy person' or 'the environmental guy' as serious play in virtually figured worlds. The play is serious because of the investment in shaping the selves they want to take back out into the wild. The students were positioning themselves within distributed communities which would offer sustained feedback after they had left the campus. Yet at the same time they were able to try out their new identities in the 'now' and 'here' of college dinners and coffee rooms.

The study has captured the students' experiences of what Vygotskians call the social situation of their development, and in particular how they are acting on and shaping it. They were creating sites of self-authoring which owed little to the social situations of development offered by the university, and at least some of their learning was evidenced in changing relationships within those extramural developmental opportunities. These observations could have been made of the generations of students who have brought strong cultural and social capital to their studies. But the opportunities for the systematic creation of personal learning environments afforded by digital media do create new disturbances in the long-established practices of higher education.

In Russ's study we witness, in a university context, some of the social transformations that are already accompanying a digitally-driven knowledge culture: where the client is positioned as a developer alongside the computer scientist; or where, as we see here, the consumer of educational support services becomes the producer. Russ's conclusion is that as students break away from university-based communities of learners, cultivate globally distributed funds of knowledge and generate virtually figured worlds, they become less dependent on learning media and communities of academic practice.

Where does that leave universities? Should we respond to fund-raising appeals for new libraries? Or should we convert existing libraries into more dining spaces and coffee areas where students' web-supported projective identities might be tested? Without a doubt there are implications for how universities organise their physical resources to play their part in supporting students' learning. However, I think there are also serious implications here for what it means to be a member of an academic community, for the capacity for sustained argument and the rigorous testing of ideas against alternative explanations. The communities inhabited by the young scholars in the study were comfortable places where they could take forward their desired identities and which they could help shape through their contributions, but they were in the end relatively narrow and specialist. What Russ termed 'globally distributed funds of knowledge' may mean that the knowledge available in these communities is widespread, but it may still be narrowly focused and rarely open to external critique.

I suggest that we in universities need to gently disrupt the identity-protecting boundaries that the students have created round their carefully constructed personal learning environments. We should entice them out into playing in the rough and tumble to be found in the figured worlds of debate and disputation that will call into question some of the safe activities and practices they are building around themselves. This is not a call for rugged individualism but for a recognition that serious play in virtually figured worlds may be as limiting as it is alluring.

Acknowledgements

This book is the end result of a long journey through my doctoral studies at Oxford and post-doctoral studies at MIT and I owe a debt of gratitude to all who have helped me along the way. Professor John Furlong and Professor Anne Edwards supervised my doctoral studies and provided an enduring source of support and encouragement throughout this journey. John helped me to believe in the wider significance of my early ethnographic case studies and encouraged me to pursue a research agenda that seemed less than conventional at the time. Later Anne equipped me with an arsenal of conceptual tools that have transformed the way I think about learning and spent hours helping me transform piles of field notes, memos and outlines into a coherent doctoral thesis. Without her patience, wisdom and understanding this book would not have been possible.

Professor Henry Jenkins has provided a major source of inspiration throughout much of this journey. Henry's essays on *Fans, Bloggers and Gamers* helped me understand why we should look to the margins to glimpse the future and his seminal work, *Convergence Culture: Where Old and New Media Collide*, helped me understand the challenges and choices confronting university students in relation to a much broader process of cultural change. I am particularly grateful to Henry for giving me the opportunity to study at MIT's Comparative Media Studies in 2005 and for taking time out of his busy schedule in the Spring of 2009 to provide detailed feedback on drafts on each chapter. The conversations we had during this time continue to inspire me.

Dr Kim Ochs acted as my mentor, friend and counsellor throughout this journey and stepped in at the eleventh hour to help me edit and proof that final manuscript. I cannot thank Kim enough for giving so generously of her time during the final stages of the writing process.

For a book concerned with learning beyond formal educational contexts it seems particularly important to acknowledge the debt of gratitude I owe to a distributed networked of informal learning companions. Howard Noble, David White and Ken Kahn stimulated and provoked my thinking during dozens of lunchtime conversations and a constant exchange of URLs throughout my time at Oxford. On the other side of the pond Ravi

Purotshotma and, later, Katie Clinton and Jenna McWilliams challenged and provoked me with their 'gloves off' critical feedback in a Davis Square coffee shop. More recently, Fred Garnett welcomed me into the Learner Generated Context research community and provided some extremely valuable support, encouragement and guidance during the final stages of the writing process. Collectively, their passion for understanding the implications of media change have spurred me on and helped these ideas grow and flourish.

I am also deeply grateful to Professor Bridget Somekh and Dr Geoff Haywood who examined my doctoral thesis. Their detailed critical feedback challenged me to embark upon the process of writing my first book. In addition, I would like to thank Dr Nick Hopwood, Dr Viv Ellis, Professor Kathy Sylva, Professor Geoffrey Walford, Dr Adam Leftstein, Dr Ioanna Kinti, Dr Amar Dhand and Dr Eric Tucker, Professor Richard Pring, Dr David Mills, Dr Peter Goodyear, Dr Stuart Lee and Professor Anne Watson. The conversations that we've had over the years continue to shape the way I think about learning and the purpose of educational research.

On a personal level I owe a debt of gratitude to Drum, Eric and Margaret Richardson, Graham Francis, Paddy Coulter, Jeff King, Julika Efurt, John Hanson, James and Mo Theodosius, Sean and Ailsa Mahoney, Angela Aristidou, Julia and Angela Cake, Bob Meldrum and Keely Flint. In addition I would like to thank: Lor Symaco, Anna Touloumakos, Gill Boag-Munroe, Sue Cranmer, Juss Kaur, Anne Geniets, Kate Lindsey, Elena Soucacou, Eleni Stamou, Jing Jing Zang, Sara Loosemore, Erica Oakes, Liz Masterman, Junko Iida, Margaret Loney, Colleen Kauman, Tuukka Toivonen, Dominic Brown and Michael Perrie for their friendship and support.

Last but not least, I would like to thank all my informants for letting me into the back regions of their everyday lives and showing me what they get up to on the Internet.

Acknowledgement of copyright permissions

I would also like to thank David White at Oxford University's Department of Technology Assisted Life Long Learning for the reuse of Figure 1.1 and Dr Thomas Malloy at the University of Utah for the reuse of the screenshot used in Figure 3.1.

Introduction

At the age of 14, as happens with many young people, Isaac reached a point as an artist where he was frustrated with his ability to produce work good enough to meet his own increasingly sophisticated and demanding standards. But the computer gave him a second chance. With the scanner, his art-tablet, *Adobe Photoshop* and other drawing, drafting, and rendering software (*Morph*, *Kai's power tools*, *Photoshop*, *Alien Skin*) Isaac was able to produce digital images of a very high quality. Isaac's web pages quickly grew in size and sophistication. A year after getting his first Internet account (a student account at $20 a month), Isaac had authored 20 pages and subpages on the e-mail messages to individuals and to the 40K list. He had become a War-hammer 40K celebrity, renowned for his e-mail prolificness, wit, and know-ledge, and for the quality of his computer graphics. Over the course of the year he had become, before our eyes, a Warhammer-otaku.

(Tobin 1998: 133)

Joseph Tobin's (1998) ethnographic case study *An American Otaku* describes how Isaac, his fourteen-year-old son, spent his time developing and manag-ing a website for fans of the Warhammer video game. It illustrates how Isaac uses a variety of digital tools to create artwork to professional standards. It shows how new media empowered Isaac to mobilize an online community of Warhammer enthusiasts and leverage the knowledge and expertise of more experienced peers if and when required. Significantly, Isaac remains wholly committed to this self-appointed role despite the absence of any kind of external rewards. The reputation of a '40K celebrity' that he acquires among this globally distributed community of Warhammer fans provides sufficient motivation. Indeed, he feels that the identity he enacts within the context of the Warhammer fan fiction community is an expression of his true self, an identity that remains repressed within the restrictive context of formal schooling.

In a comparable case study entitled, *Why Heather Can Write*, Henry Jenkins (2006c) describes how Heather, a thirteen-year-old girl, becomes the teen editor of *The Daily Prophet*, an online newspaper produced by a globally distributed network of *Harry Potter* fans. Heather 'hires columnists who cover their own beats', 'edits stories in preparation for publication', and 'consults on issues of style and grammar' (p. 171). In short, Heather acquires a range of editorial, networking and managerial skills in the process of enacting a self-appointed role. For, Jenkins this case study becomes a powerful emblem of the new opportunities for self-directed learning afforded by young people's expanding access to the Internet. Further, it suggests how a young person might acquire a range of new media literacies, conceived as the social skills and cultural competences required to become a full participant in an emerging media landscape (Jenkins *et al.* 2006). Interestingly, Heather is not conscious of the fact she is learning and developing skills that have become invaluable in the information age. She learns to use the tools, resources and masters the communicative practices required to enact her responsibilities through practice. The activity appears motivated by the authentic feedback, respect and acknowledgement she receives from a distributed community of Harry Potter fans as she cultivates a global network of fan fiction writers to staff *The Daily Prophet*.

When I first read these case studies as a graduate student, I was struck by the way they opened a window onto a world of intrinsically motivated creativity and self-directed learning made possible by young people's expanding access to the Internet. They suggest why we need to look beyond the use of information and communication technologies (ICTs) in formal educational contexts to understand the real implications of media change for learning. Furthermore, I believe they hint at some of the ways resourceful individuals are breaking away from traditional modes of learning and instruction, taking control and designing quasi-virtual ecologies that empower them to pursue lifelong learning agendas relatively independently of formal educational institutions.

Both case studies also draw attention to the way these learners generate quasi-virtual contexts that function as spaces of self-authoring. Understanding this process demands a dialectical way of thinking. Winston Churchill once wrote: 'We shape our buildings that then thereafter shape us'.[1] In many ways this quotation encapsulates the dialectical movement I attempt to unpack throughout this book. I am not, however, concerned with physical buildings made of bricks and mortar. I am interested in the ways advanced learners are designing and cultivating quasi-virtual ecologies, or *virtually figured worlds*, that in turn shape their sense of who they are and who they might become. In this respect, the book aims to explore how learners are exploiting access to the Internet to take more control over their own developmental trajectories through life.

These insights certainly resonate with my own experience of growing up through a period of rapid media change. My earliest recollections of school involved inkwells, blotting paper, wooden rulers and reciting multiplication tables that the teacher had scrawled across a blackboard with a piece of chalk. I had no agency in this environment. All the props and scaffolds were imposed from the outside. As a result, I rarely felt invested in the tasks at hand. In contrast, when at home, I frequently found myself deeply engaged in a variety of playful, creative and exploratory learning activities. For example, I remember investing hours writing computer programs in Visual Basic and frequently stayed up late into the night playing complex and challenging games like Civilization III and Sim City 3000. I rarely engaged in these activities alone. I played with friends, discussing strategies and tactics as we played. Occasionally I co-opted the expertise of my father to help with specific problems as they arose. In short, within the home context I was relatively free to create, discover and actively manage the level of assistance required to solve problems.

As a teenager I taught myself to play the guitar and started to build a home recording studio. In this space I felt free to create, discover and play out my rock star fantasies. By the time I was nineteen, it integrated a primitive Tascam four track, a digital drum machine, effects pedals, a midi keyboard and a digital sequencer called Cubase Audio, which I installed on a chunky old desktop PC. Indeed, my hybrid digital-analogue home studio empowered me to create and record high quality multi-track compositions and burn them to a CD-ROM. I never became a rock star, but I feel as if this space nurtured latent creative impulses and helped me believe I could pursue a career in the creative industries. In this respect, this quasi-virtual ecology started to function as a space of self-authoring.

Today I am attempting to write these words on a 2.0 GHz laptop loaded with dozens of digital tools (Word, Endnote, Atlas.ti to name but a few) in a radically personalized media environment that I have designed and cultivated over the years. This virtually figured world now integrates dozens of quick links to listservs, RSS feeds, blogs, wikis and social networking tools that mediate every aspect of the way I think, learn, create and communicate with people interested in digital media and learning from around the world. More recently, I have found myself following media theorists on Twitter, building a globally distributed network of professional contacts on LinkedIn, sharing video podcasts of inspirational lectures on Facebook and publishing PowerPoint presentations on Slideshare. In short, I have become a post-human cyborg learner utterly dependent on this finely tuned cognitive ecology – which I have grown to understand as my extended mind – that helps me write, plan, think, visualize, organize my ideas, disseminate my work and gain critical feedback on ideas from people around the world. To an ever-increasing extent my capacity to participate in academic life appears to depend upon the configuration of this virtually figured world. Indeed, I have engaged in the process of writing this book at home, in my study room, in libraries, in coffee shops and in airport departure lounges. As a result, I feel less and less dependent on resources and communities supported by the traditional university.

This book builds on these insights. It attempts to explore how students, left to their own devices, are creatively appropriating digital tools and resources to study, learn and play. I focus on the practices of postgraduate students with whom I lived in an Oxford college. I have learnt a great deal from this group. As a research student I spent hours hanging out in college dorms in an attempt to find out what they were getting up to on the Internet. In the years that followed I never ceased to be surprised by what I saw and what they told me. Early case studies revealed students discovering and using interactive web-based tutorials to teach themselves statistics and advertising their changing moods through the posting of away messages. In time, I discovered students designing sophisticated virtual environments to facilitate brain image analysis, using Wikipedia to prepare for job interviews and conducting exploratory literature searches with the aid of the Amazon. com book recommendations system. Towards the end of the study I became interested in the ways advanced students were taking on professional roles and responsibilities as they enacting the roles of environmental activists, political campaigners and human rights consultants as they engaged with online culture.

Despite my interest in these emergent practices, I often found myself struggling to find the right words to conceptualize and describe what I observed. The problem was compounded by the rapidity of media change. When attempting to justify my proposed scheme of study I argued that the digitally mediated practices of graduate students could provide a grounded insight into what it meant to be literate in the new media age. In time I became more interested in the ways learners were breaking away from centralized services and designing radically personalized learning environments that they took with them as they moved across countries and institutional contexts. With the emergence of Web 2.0 and the widespread uptake of social software technologies like MSN Messenger and Facebook, I became interested in the ways students were cultivating globally distributed personal networks and mobilizing the knowledge and skills of remote learning companions to tackle specific problems. More recently, I have become interested in understanding how new media empowers individuals to take on professional roles and responsibilities and take more control over their developmental trajectories in life. These themes co-exist and unfold throughout this book. However, they are brought together under the umbrella notion that as a result of media change we have witnessed the decentring of the traditional university. This way of thinking demands that we start to map out an emergent arena of self-directed web-based learning activity that transcends institutional boundaries. Further, it requires that we start to think of learners' identities as powerful mediators and motivators of self-directed learning activity.

A key challenge is to develop a new language for thinking about this emergent culture of self-directed learning activity. Each chapter attempts to advance this overall project. To orientate the reader the following section provides a brief overview of the contents of each chapter.

Chapter 1: From the culture industry to participatory culture

Chapter 1 works at a macro level and orientates the reader to a way of understanding the implications of media change for learning and education. It illustrates how an emergent web-based 'participatory culture' (Jenkins 2006a) has started to converge or collide with top-down 'culture industry' (Adorno 1975) model of education that inhibits learning agency and restricts access to knowledge. Today's learners find themselves in a predicament as they struggle to navigate personalized learning trajectories that combine the old with the new. I argue that ethnographic studies that explore informal learning, creativity and play in digital subcultures have started to open up a window onto the new learning opportunities afforded and help us in understanding the interrelationships between learning, motivation, play and identity in an emerging media landscape. Further, I argue that research focused on the practices of university students can advance this field of inquiry and provide unique insights into the real implications for media change for the future of (self) education.

Chapter 2: Cognitive anthropology on the Cyberian frontier

Chapter 2 introduces the reader to the central tenets of sociocultural theory and explains why this tradition provides a powerful conceptual toolkit for investigating emergent learning practices in an emerging media landscape. In particular, it illustrates why an approach inspired by Vygotsky's genetic method provides a method for investigating how learners appropriate digital tools and resources to expand learning opportunities and address authentic learning needs. Engeström's (1987) theory of 'expansive learning', Dorothy Holland *et al.*'s (1998) work on 'figured worlds' and James Paul Gee's (2004) work on 'projective identities' are identified as particularly useful conceptual tools for advancing this line of inquiry. This chapter also explains why a sociocultural approach can help us develop a grounded insight in some advanced new media literacies in action. In multiple respects Chapter 2 lays the conceptual foundations for the theory building project that unfolds throughout the remainder of the book. Chapters 3 through 6 unpack and develop the insights offered with reference to examples that illustrate students' everyday use of digital tools and resources.

Chapter 3: The learner as designer

Chapter 3 explores some of the ways students are designing radically personalized learning environments to support advanced knowledge work. It moves beyond the notion of 'distributed cognition' and 'cognitive offloading' as metaphors for understanding the mind expanding powers of digital tools and foregrounds the concept of 'design', conceived as a capacity to impose control from the outside. One vignette describes how Tim, a student of psychiatry used a freely downloadable Multiple Desktop Powertool to design a virtual desktop environment that facilitated the process of analysing brain scan images. The argument stresses that a capacity to *mindfully* design a radically personalized mediascape for advanced knowledge work has become a fundamental aspect of new media literacy. However it also highlights emerging tensions and contradictions as the distinctions between virtual study space and recreational space begins to break down.

Chapter 4: Creative appropriation, new media and (self) education

Chapter 4 explores some of the ways learners are *creatively appropriating* digital tools and web-based resources in combination with resources administered by centralized library and information services. The discussion is developed with reference to the work of Jim Wertsch (1998), Mikhail Bakhtin (1981) and Michel de Certeau (1988) and descriptive vignettes that illustrate some of the surprising and unexpected ways students are using digital tools to address authentic learning needs. For example, one vignette describes how a student using the Amazon.com book recommendation system to conduct exploratory literature searches gained an insight into the multiple 'webs of influence' among authors. Overall, this chapter suggests that students are now breaking away from a dependence on the traditional university and turning to the Internet as a primary resource for learning and self-instruction.

Chapter 5: Globally distributed funds of living knowledge

Chapter 5 directs the reader's attention to some of the ways students are exploiting social software to learn with others through new media. Building on conceptual work by Bonnie A. Nardi *et al.* (2002), Luis Moll *et al.* (1992, 1997) and Anne Edwards (2005), this chapter illustrates how learners are cultivating, nurturing and activating *globally distributed funds of living knowledge* to address specific learning needs. For example, one vignette shows how a student nurtured her personal network by the posting of away messages on MSN Messenger and later leveraged the expertise of two critical friends who lived 'back home in California' to provide detailed critical feedback on her dissertation on the death penalty. The discussion draws attention to the way a well-nurtured *globally distributed fund of living knowledge* might empower students to solve problems, negotiate career moves and gain access to the professions.

Chapter 6: Learning through serious play in virtually figured worlds

Chapter 6 explores some of the ways advanced students are learning through *serious play in virtually figured worlds* that allow them to take on professional roles and responsibilities. Building on the work of Jerome Bruner (1991), Sherry Turkle (1997), James Paul Gee (2004) and Dorothy Holland *et al.* (1998) it offers a constellation of conceptual tools: *virtually figured worlds, committed learning, identity in digitally mediated practice* and *history in laptop* that can help us understand this process. Overall, this chapter helps us understand how advanced learners are transforming the quasi-virtual contexts of their own learning and personal development. It concludes by exploring how a virtually figured world might function as an *expanded space of self-authoring* that empowers young people to explore possible future selves and possible future career trajectories. Of all the chapters, I believe this one provides the deepest insight into the future of (self) education.

Chapter 7: The decentring of the traditional university

Chapter 7 engages with a wider debate in the literature and proposes a model for conceptualizing the implications of media change for higher education at a systemic level. An activity theoretical model is used to conceptualize the predicament of the learner caught up in this process of cultural transition. This model suggests that systemic change in higher education is now driven from the bottom-up as millions of students across the world turn to the Internet as their primary learning resource. Finally this model encourages us to understand the journey through higher education as an identity-project in which students work on their projective identities as they engage in both formal and informal activities. In turn, these observations suggest that we are now witnessing the decentring of the traditional university in the everyday lives of students. Indeed, the discussion suggests that we have indeed entered a period of profound and historic change in the culture of higher education that requires us to reconceptualize how, why, where and with whom learning takes place. The chapter concludes by suggesting directions for further research and hints at how a developmental research agenda could empower all students to exploit the full potential of the Internet as a resource for (self) education.

1 From the culture industry to participatory culture

Deliberate learning involves engaging with the exposition, orchestrated discussion, research, systematic annotation, the focused reading of text, and a variety of other directed activities that many students may not always find easy to mobilize and manage independently. Sites of formal education have evolved structures that sustain and coordinate such activities with a scaffold of cultural resources: timetables, curricular, designed spaces, discourse rituals, and so on.

(Crook and Light 2002: 158)

But what happens when learners gain access to tools and resources that afford new opportunities to learn which are not dependent on the traditional structures of formal education? This book investigates the various ways learners are now appropriating digital tools and resources to break away from traditional modes of learning and instruction and advancing radically personalized learning agendas in quasi-virtual contexts of their own figuration.

Understanding media change: from the culture industry to participatory culture

To illuminate what I perceive as the central shift in the locus of agency for managing and regulating learning it is helpful to understand why the once-dominant trope of the culture industry (associated with mid-twentieth century conceptions of mass media culture) has given way to the trope of participatory culture (associated with new media). Used as conceptual tools, I believe these tropes can direct the attention of educationalists to some of the most significant implications of media change for learning, cognition and the future of education.

The culture industry is a term that acquired meaning in the work of Adorno and Horkheimer (1972) to describe a monolithic, centralized and top-down mode of cultural production.[1] For Adorno (1975), traditional expressions of popular culture such as the folk ballad percolated upwards from grassroots communities and, therefore, expressed the sentiments, anxieties and aspirations of ordinary people. In contrast, the products of the culture industry are 'commodities through and through', manufactured, marketed and sold, like hamburgers, at passive consumers 'more or less according to a plan' (p. 31). A model that has parallels in what Freire (1985) described as a transmission or 'piggy bank' model of education in which knowledge is deposited into empty vessels. From this perspective, the production and consumption of cultural products cannot be considered independently from strategies of power and control. Indeed, Adorno asserts that 'the culture industry intentionally integrates its consumers from above' (1975: 31). The implication is that post-industrial society is profoundly dehumanizing; a sentiment expressed in dozens of statements. For example, Adorno argues: 'the concoctions of the culture industry are neither guides for a blissful life, nor a new art of moral responsibility, but rather exhortations to toe the line, behind which stand the most powerful interests' (p. 36).

The grand theorizing of these Frankfurt School theorists engages in a political and ideological debate in which the mass media are conceptualized as obstacles to achieving a more democratic, just and equitable society. Today, with the benefit of hindsight, these somewhat melodramatic discourses – characterized by the recurrent themes of victimization, subjugation and manipulation – read like politically motivated post-Marxist 'critical pessimism', very much a product of its time, designed to highlight the enduring inequalities and exploitation of late capitalism. Nevertheless, whether one agrees or not with the anti-enlightenment invective, the work of the Frankfurt School theorists captures something essential about the centralization of power and state control over knowledge and culture that occurred in the mid-twentieth century.

Adorno's critique of a top-down centralized culture industry resonates in a post-Marxist critique of centralized education systems and formal schooling. For example, in *Learning to Labour: How Working Class Kids Get Working Class Jobs*, Willis (1978) depicts a group of working class 'lads' in a British secondary modern school resisting and rejecting the values of their middle class teachers. Instead they embrace the working class values of their lifeworld communities but thereby condemn themselves to a life of hard manual labour. Significantly, within the culture that Willis describes, access to knowledge, qualifications and the professions are regulated and controlled by a centralized establishment. Further, the hierarchical and regimented structures of formal schooling appear designed to diminish the 'lads'' ties with folk culture, craft apprenticeships and informal modes of community learning. In this respect, a culture industry model of education is profoundly dehumanizing and diminishes learner agency. Nevertheless, not all theorists – not even those working within a post-Marxist paradigm – have bought into the culture industry metaphor.

Enzensberger (2004 [1974]) argues that 'Marxists have not understood the *consciousness* industry and have been aware only of its bourgeois-capitalist dark-side and not of its socialist possibilities' (p. 82).[2] For Enzensberger, the 'open secret of the electronic media, the decisive political factor – which has been waiting, suppressed or crippled, for its moment to come – is their mobilizing power' (p. 69).[3] He is referring to the first generation of electronic media: 'news satellites, colour television, cable relay television, cassettes, videotape, videotape recorders, video phones, stereophony, laser techniques, electrostatic reproduction processes, electronic high speed printing ...' (p. 68). For Enzensberger the new electronic media are constantly forming new kinds of connections both with each other and with older media like printing, radio and film, and quite unlike the mass media that inform Adorno's culture industry. The central thrust of his argument is to debunk the 'possibility of total control of such a system' (p. 70). For Enzensberger the new electronic media are making possible mass participation in a 'social and socialized productive process, the practical means of which are in the hands of the masses themselves' (p. 69).

From this perspective, the content and meanings transmitted are controlled from the centre through media like television and film deny the possibility of an exchange between transmitter and receiver. In radio, however, Enzensberger foresees the new possibilities:

> Radio would be the most wonderful means of communication imaginable in public life, a huge linked system – that is to say, it would be such if it were capable not only of transmitting but of receiving, of allowing the listener not only to hear but to speak, and did not isolate him but brought him into contact.
>
> (Enzensberger 2004 [1974]: 70)

His comments seem almost ludicrously utopian. However, these words appear to anticipate the vision that has inspired many attempting to develop social and participatory media forms that allow individuals to create, share and communicate with others around the world.

In *Technologies of Freedom*, Pool (1983) makes a similar case. For Pool the media itself is neutral. Yet, when the means of communication are 'decentralized' and made 'easily available', they can be appropriated by marginal groups to serve diverse agendas:

> Freedom is fostered when the means of communication are dispersed, decentralized, and easily available, as are printing presses or microcomputers. Central control is more likely when the means of communication are concentrated, monopolized, and scarce, as are great networks.
>
> (Pool 1983: 11)

In this respect, he foresaw that new media would become a site of struggle as different groups attempted to appropriate the means of communication and dissemination of information for their own ends.

The notion of a culture as a 'site of struggle' between the dominant and dispossessed is central to the thinking of Raymond Williams (1961, 1983, 2003) and the Birmingham School of Cultural Studies.[4] For example, a group of cultural theorists collected in *Resistance through Rituals* (Hall and Jefferson 1976) highlight the diverse ways that the disempowered groups, particularly post-war youth subcultures, resisted being subjugated by a hegemonic establishment. These theorists attempt to understand how grass-roots 'folk' cultures maintain a distinctive cultural identity, appropriating, subverting and resisting the available semiotic resources to resist the values of the establishment. Interestingly, in the work of media theorist Henry Jenkins, this mode of thinking has become important for understanding the role of new media, new technologies and community formation in the age of the Internet.[5]

Jenkins charts the evolution of the mediascape through successive phases of technological innovation that correspond to the titles of his three seminal works. *Textual Poachers: Television Fans and Participatory Culture* (Jenkins 1992) explores the practice of TV fans as they sample and remix video footage from popular TV series like *Star Trek* to retell stories from marginal or deviant perspectives. In this volume fan fiction is produced invariably for comic effect and remains confined to a niche subcultural practice. In *Fans, Bloggers and Gamers: Exploring Participatory Culture* Jenkins (2006b) discusses how fans start to appropriate digital technologies to 'poach', rework, and share creative work over the World Wide Web. In this collection, we see grassroots activists appropriating blogging technologies to challenge the authority of traditional print-based newspapers and the emergence of new practices, such as 'ad-busting', that threaten the hegemony of corporate rule.[6] In short, participatory culture signifies a world in which audiences start to play an active role in shaping, subverting and remaking the media they consume. In his latest work *Convergence Culture: Where Old and New Media Collide*, Jenkins (2006a) starts to conceptualize a media environment in which audience participation is recognized and embraced as valuable resource. In this respect convergence culture might be regarded as the dialectical synthesis of culture industry and participatory culture. From this perspective, the tensions and contradictions that characterize convergence culture are somewhat inevitable.

The central movement is to chart the rise of participatory culture from the margins to the mainstream, from the subcultural skirmishes with the culture industry, typically described using metaphors of 'poaching' or 'pilfering', to a 'central resource' that might be used to mobilize the voters in a presidential campaign. Indeed, as participatory culture moves from the periphery to the centre it becomes a cultural force to be reckoned with, a force that established institutions can no longer afford to ignore. Moreover, participatory culture threatens to disrupt the revenue streams, political structures and laws regulating media consumption upon which the power of these institutions depend. The devastating effect that the Napster and

Kazaar file-sharing communities had on the record industry supports this thesis (Battelle 2006). Further evidence might be discerned through an analysis of the panicked reaction of the telecommunications industry to the sudden appearance of Skype.

The rise and enormous popularity of Web 2.0 technologies such as Wikipedia, My Space, Friendster, Flickr and Facebook tend to support Jenkins' claims. These tools support the sharing of user generated content and the formation of thousands of online special interest groups. Statistics confirm that the use of Wikipedia (the free online encyclopedia produced and edited by its own users) have rocketed whilst use of Encarta (Microsoft's leading commercial online encyclopedia) has gradually declined (Madden and Fox 2006: 3). Similarly, statistical data that illustrate the massive popularity of social software sites tend to confirm the trend. Indeed, Madden and Fox (2006: 5) argue that 'the beating heart of the Internet has always been its ability to leverage our social connections', adding 'social networking sites like My Space, Facebook and Friendster struck a powerful social chord at the right time with the right technology'.

The broader impact of these cultural shifts is widespread yet uncertain. For Jenkins, no institution appears unaffected. He highlights the way digital technologies empower ordinary consumers to archive, annotate, appropriate and re-circulate media content. As a consequence he argues that: 'Powerful institutions and practices (law, religion, education, advertising, and politics, among them) are being redefined by a growing recognition of what is to be gained through fostering – or at least tolerating – participatory cultures' (Jenkins 2006a: 2). Jenkins' conceptualization of the tensions driving media change provides a powerful model for thinking through the challenges confronting education. It leads one to understand media change as a site of struggle between an emergent web-based participatory culture that affords a variety of informal learning opportunities and the top-down hierarchical structures of formal educational institutions (including schools, libraries and universities) that are now attempting to take stock. The challenge, for the researcher, is to understand the various ways media franchises, governments, business and educational institutions are attempting to contain or assimilate the rise of participatory cultures.

Literature that explores some of the implications of media change for education reveals how some of the tensions and contradictions are now manifest in the everyday experiences and practices of learners of all ages.

Media change and learning

The debate about the implications of media change for learning has tended to move from celebratory treatments that highlight the new learning opportunities afforded by young people's expanding access to the Internet to more measured treatments that emphasize the challenges and choices confronting learners. For example, in *The Rise of the Net Generation* Tapscott's (1998)

'N-Geners' are constructed as a uniformly capable, responsible and resourceful generation. They are inquisitive and curious when venturing into the brave new online world that contains 'much of the world's knowledge', 'millions of peers', and 'thrilling, enchanting and bizarre new experiences'. Indeed, the 'Net' is constructed as a utopian medium that might be regarded as an educational 'good' in every respect: 'Time spent on the net is not passive time, it's active time. It's reading time. It's investigation time. It's skill development and problem solving time. It's time analysing and evaluating. It's composing your thoughts time. It's writing time' (Tapscott 1998: 7).

Survey studies have debunked some of the more utopian claims made by advocates of a uniform digital generation. Indeed, they draw our attention to the need to treat many of the claims made with caution. For example, interpreting the findings of a national survey called *UK Children Go Online*, Livingstone and Bober (2004) argue:

> Children and young people are divided into those for whom the Internet is an increasingly rich, diverse, engaging and stimulating resource or growing importance in their lives, and those for whom it remains a narrow, unengaging if occasionally useful resource of rather less significance.
>
> (Livingstone and Bober 2004: 5)

Later White's (2007) Spire Project Survey had highlighted the fact that people (of all ages) are now exploiting the affordances of emerging technologies like Wikipedia, YouTube, Skype, MSN Messenger and Second Life for a mixture of work, study, socializing and fun activities (see Figure 1.1). A key challenge for educational researchers has been to better understand how and why learners actually use these tools and resources in everyday life to support learning.

The most powerful studies in this field draw attention to the complex relationships between learning, motivation, identity and play in an emerging media landscape. For example, Facer *et al.* (2003) draw attention to the way a schoolboy called David grew into the role of the family ICT expert and was frequently called upon at school by teachers to sort out computer problems, and describe Karen's frustrated attempts to use the Internet to find out about 'Welsh love spoons' for her technology homework (p. 159). Significantly, children's informal use of digital technologies appears driven by pre-existing interests. For example, Facer *et al.* (2003) describe how Jamilia and her friends, who surfed the Internet to find out more about Asian fashion, used the web to construct a modern Anglo-Asian identity. These choices appear motivated by pre-existing interests that relate to learners' emerging sense of self and community.

Significantly, for Facer *et al.* (2003) the free, exploratory and playful ways young people are engaging with ICTs in the home appear increasingly out of step with the restricted ways children are able to use ICTs within the

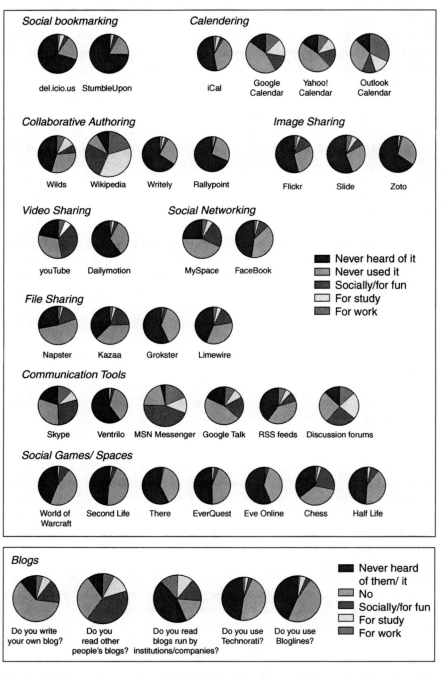

Figure 1.1 Proportionate use of Web 2.0 tools for socializing, study and work-related activities (source: White 2007).

institutional context of school. Indeed, a key distinction between the learning in and out of school is framed in terms of choice. At home, young people were free to choose what they wanted to use the computer for. Moreover, learning to use computers and various software tools was rarely perceived as an end in itself. Young people acquired knowledge, skills and technical proficiencies in the process of using the computer to do something that they wanted to do. For this reason the authors are sceptical of blanket statements like computers 'make your children more creative' or 'make your children smarter' and argue that learning with computers is a much more complex matter, involving an interaction between child, technology and the specific sociocultural contexts.

From this perspective a capacity to monopolize on the new opportunities afforded appears highly dependent on a range of contextual factors. Moreover, these observations direct us to investigate exactly how, why and for what purposes learners are making use of the Internet. Finally, they suggest that we are more likely to find evidence of really innovative practice when we explore people's use of the Internet outside of formal educational contexts where learners are free to follow their own agendas.

In *Adult Learning in the Digital Age*, Selwyn *et al.* (2006) note that only a small minority of adults were using the Internet to engage in taught online courses. In contrast, many had started to use the Internet to develop their own hobbies and interests. Indeed, this seemed far more significant. They authors argue:

> It seems that much of the ICT-supported informal learning documented in our study took the specific form of 'self education' – a more specific and personalised form of informal learning concerned primarily with the individual's ongoing and burgeoning relationship with knowledge.
>
> (Selwyn *et al.* 2006: 183)

Again this work encourages us to understand how individual learners are appropriating digital tools and resources for self-directed learning that appears motivated by their own values and priorities rather than those foisted upon them by a structured curriculum. Further, these observations highlight the need to map out and conceptualize this emergent sphere of self-directed learning activity.

Progressive ethnographic research that explores young people's informal uses of new media has started to provide new categories and typologies for understanding emergent learning practices mediated by digital tools and resources. For example, in a recent large scale ethnographic study reported in *Living and Learning with New Media*, Ito *et al.* (2008) draw a useful distinction between 'friendship driven' practices and 'interest driven' practices. Under the rubric of 'friendship driven practices' the authors chart the various ways young people 'mess around' and 'hang out' with friends in 'networked publics' supported by social software technologies like My Space and

Facebook. These *genres* of participation are not particularly new to the digital domain. Nevertheless, digital media and 'always-on' Internet connectivity appears to extend opportunities to play, tinker, experiment, hang out and mess around with friends in distributed communities. In contrast, 'geeking out' is offered as a category to describe the way some young people are engaging with media and technology in an intense, autonomous and interests-driven way. Moreover, 'geeking out' is regarded as a unique feature of today's media environment. The authors describe the practice in the following terms:

> Geeking out involves learning to navigate esoteric domains of knowledge and practice and participating in communities that traffic in these forms of expertise. It is a mode of learning that is peer-driven, but focused on gaining deep knowledge and expertise in specific areas of interest.
>
> (Ito *et al.* 2008: 28)

Interestingly the authors' use of the term is stretched far beyond its traditional associations with computer geeks. Rather, it draws attention to the way young people are accessing specialist knowledge in a variety of domains and connecting with others who share their interests and passions from around the world regardless of age, class or cultural background. As an analytic tool the term 'geeking out' encourages researchers to explore how and why some individuals are developing deeply committed self-directed learning agendas through pro-active participation with online culture.

Taken together, these studies do more than describe the learning opportunities afforded by new media and a burgeoning variety of online communities. They suggest that an emergent culture of informal learning supported by ICTs might constitute what Coffield (2000: 1–10) has described as the 'structure below the surface' that accounts for two-thirds of learning despite the fact that it remains largely unseen. This book attempts to probe this emerging sphere of learning activity and offer new conceptual tools that might help us better understand it. It does not negate the continuing importance of schools, universities, lectures, seminars and accredited courses that offer more formalized and structured learning opportunities. However the culture I describe does provide an insight into the disjuncture between course-related study and self education, a disjuncture that is nowhere more conspicuous than in studies focused on the changing practices of college students.

Peering into the future of (self) education

College students have been constructed as a unique population who occupy the 'middle ground between childhood and adulthood, between work and leisure and who have been at the forefront of social change since the end of

World War II' (Jones 2002: 5). Indeed, unlike schools or homes, college cultures appear to facilitate the rapid diffusion of innovative practice that later trickle down to the wider population. For example Jones (2002) draws attention to the way many Internet tools, such as Yahoo and Napster, and practices such as file-sharing, blogging, social-networking and Internet telephony were developed by and for college students. Similar observations lead Mcmillan and Morrison (2006: 74) to argue: 'understanding of how new technology is influencing the various domains of these young people's lives provides a window on what Internet use may be like for future generations'.

To date, only a handful of studies have attempted to understand how media change is experienced and impacts upon the everyday life practices of college students beyond formal educational settings. Crook and Light's (2002) *The Cultural Practice of Study* provides a theoretically sophisticated treatment. The authors are vehemently critical of liberationalist language that uncritically celebrates the virtualization of learning in the networked university. Indeed, they position themselves in opposition to the likes of Blustein *et al.* (1999: 156) who have argued 'when students can get cash at 2 AM, download library materials at 3 AM, and order shoes from L.L. Bean at 4 AM, it is only educational inertia that keeps them convinced that they must learn calculus by sitting in the same classroom for fifty minutes, three times a week'. Crook and Light argue that manifestos of this type imply that opportunities to study should be as accessible and consumer-friendly as opportunities to shop. In contrast they adopt a somewhat conservative stance and argue: 'learning is an activity that cannot be so readily abstracted from its context' and 'calmly executed at other arbitrary times and places' (p. 156).

In general Crook and Light draw attention to the enabling constraints implicit in traditional learning environments and paper-based learning media and emphasize the need to recruit informal practices into more purposeful structured learning activities. For example, they argue: 'Successful education involves making students comfortable with the activities demanded by formal study: encouraging them to allow their repertoire of informal cultural practices – listening, talking, investigating and so on – to be formalised in ways that then support learning' (Crook and Light 2002: 174). Their work conveys a reverence for bricks and mortar institutions that have evolved over the centuries to support concentrated study. In this respect, it provides a much needed corrective to those who uncritically celebrate the new learning opportunities afforded. Nevertheless, Crook and Light adopt a somewhat lecturer-centred perspective that seems preoccupied with promoting practices and study strategies favoured by course tutors that lead students towards accredited learning outcomes. Their argument fails to take account for the reverse movement, when students intentionally break away from traditional modes of learning and instruction and seek out new opportunities to learn beyond the confines of the traditional university.

At present, the informal sphere of self-directed learning activity in the everyday lives of university students supported by a web-based participatory culture remains relatively uncharted. We do know that students are making use of their own technologies in combination with those provided by the university. Indeed, in 2006 a Higher Education Academy report noted:

> there is an increasing recognition that students are making use of their own technology as well as those provided for them and that they are doing this in ways that are not planned for, difficult to predict and may not be immediately visible to their teachers or researchers.
>
> (Sharpe *et al.* 2006: 4)

However, we do not know how ownership and use of these personal technologies are changing students' relationships with and dependence on the tools, resources and communities supported by the traditional modes of learning and self-instruction.

Research site, informants and data collection

To advance this line of inquiry from 2005 through 2007 I conducted an ethnographic study focused on the digitally mediated practices of graduate students' use of new media (Francis 2008). The following year I conducted a series of light touch but more tightly focused case studies looking more specifically at students' use of social and participatory media forms or so called Web 2.0 technologies (O'Reilly 2005).

All students recruited for the study lived in college dorms that had a fast 'always-on' Ethernet connection that gave them direct access to the university's online information services. For example, students could access the library catalogue, online journals and course materials uploaded to Web Learn (an institutional Virtual Learning Environment) directly from their study rooms. As a result, many students enjoyed a greater level of access to online resources provided by the centralized university services in their study rooms than they did in some of the university libraries. Nevertheless, access to centralized services did not appear particularly significant in students' everyday accounts of Internet use. Instead, students started to talk about their use web-based tools like Wikipedia and YouTube for a mixture of study, self-education and entertainment purposes.

Some of these tools became integrated into students' everyday lives as the study progressed. For example, many students started to use social media like MSN Messenger (and later Skype) to maintain daily contacts with friends and family members around the world and by 2007 the vast majority of students at Oxford used Facebook for a variety of social, recreational and 'just for fun' purposes. Thus in multiple respects, the context for this study constituted the intersection between the physical university, the services it provided online, and a distributed network of contacts, services and communities readily accessible on the World Wide Web.

I lived in college dorms myself throughout this period and spent hundreds of hours talking to students in and around the college about the way their everyday use of the Internet was impacting upon their everyday lives. In this respect, the insights developed in this book are informed by a sustained period of immersion in the field as a participant observer.[7] Nevertheless, the data used for illustrative purposes throughout this book focus on the practices of sixteen students who were the subjects of in-depth ethnographic case studies between 2005 and 2007. A breakdown of the final group of students is displayed in Table 1.1.

Compared to national statistics this group were high-end users of the Internet. However, it would not be accurate to conceive of the group as tech-savvy digital natives. In general these students used digital tools and resources, if and when required, to study, to advance their pre-existing hobbies and interests, to socialize and build personal friendships networks. To suggest the variety of things that students in this group were doing whilst online (apart from engaging in academic work) a table of hobbies and interests that involved the use of the Internet is reproduced in Table 1.2. This is in no way an exhaustive list. Interviews rapidly uncovered all kinds of additional activities that involved the use of the Internet. The table simply conveys the degree to which the Internet had become integrated into the fabric of everyday life. In short, these students used computers that they owned, in quasi-domestic spaces for large parts of the day, and actively exploited access to the Internet for a wide variety of purposes: to learn, make friends, network, find partners and prepare for the jump into the job market.

Table 1.1 Demographics of students recruited for the study

Pseudonym	Age	Gender	Subject	Nationality	Course
Edina	30	F	Forced Migration Studies	British	MSc
Clinton	23	M	Social Policy	American	MSc
Sue Ellen	23	F	Evidence-Based Social Work	American	MSc
Timothy	26	M	Psychiatry	British	DPhil
Ishani	23	F	Medicine	British	MD
Anastasia	28	F	Evidence-Based Social Work	Romanian	MSc
Miss Lullaby	23	F	Social Policy	American	MSc
Karen	23	F	Postgraduate Cert in Education	British	MSc
Ardash	26	M	Education/Medical Anthropology	Canadian	DPhil
Jacob	31	M	Environmental Policy	American	MSc
Jim	31	M	Law	Canadian	MSt
Katrina	26	F	Anthropology	German	MSc
Daisy D.	25	F	Medical Anthropology	American	MSc
Peter	25	M	Medical History	British	PGCE
Jacqueline	23	F	International Relations	British/French	DPhil
ZeroGBoy	25	M	Geography/Education	British	DPhil

Table 1.2 List of hobbies and interests involving the use of the Internet

Music	Internet shopping	Games
Movies	I-tunes	Burning CDs
File sharing	Instant Messenger	Playing flute
Roller Coast Tycoon	Cosmetics and fashion	Recording
Friendster	Procrastination sites	Making DVDs
Scuba diving	IQ Tests	Family tree
Quizzes	Chessbase tournaments	Chat
Organizing photos	Arranging social events	Downloading music
Photography	Current affairs	Games are for Geeks
Chess	News/politics	Arts and events in London
Relationship maintenance	Music (I-tunes)	Monitoring gender issues
Self-taught Visual Basic	File sharing	Politics and current affairs
Sharing photos	I-Pod	Watching DVDs
Ball organizing	eBaying	Downloading movies
I consider people a hobby	Hot-rodding PC	Talking to people
Gardening and food	Dating	Salsa

Data collection involved multiple qualitative or ethnographic methods. The procedure started with a series of informal conversations. Each participant who consented to take part in the study then agreed to meet in their study room at a particular time. In the first instant participants completed a questionnaire that provided demographic information and provided an overview of the Internet use. At this time notes were made about the arrangement of their computers and other resources ready-to-hand in their study rooms. Following short periods of observation I tended to ask short questions that stimulated participants to reflect upon, describe and explain their use of various tools and resources as they worked at their computers. Screenshots were often captured at this time. Each student then took part in an in-depth interview that picked up up on points made in the questionnaire and one or more stimulated response sessions. As the study progressed respondent led interviews tended to become more akin to semi-structured interviews where I used 'points to explore' lists to probe emergent themes. Data collection continued after initial analysis of the transcripts, with follow-up interviews and e-mail correspondence or additional in-depth interviews and stimulated response sessions. Short periods of *retrospective virtual ethnography* were also conducted in order to explore particular online spaces that students discussed during interview in greater depth. A full account of data collection methods and rationale used for field work is provided in the Appendix.

This mode of ethnographic inquiry produced a rich and messy data set that threw up dozens of emergent themes. At first it was almost impossible to organize or structure. However, as the study evolved I developed an interest in sociocultural and activity theory and the work of some influential cognitive anthropologists. In time, methodologically protocols and conceptual tools derived from these traditions started to guide data collection and analysis.

To orientate the general reader into a sociocultural mode of thinking, Chapter 2 provides a brief introduction to the central tenets of this tradition and proceeds to identify some important conceptual innovations that offer a powerful new way to start thinking about emergent learning practices. These tools allow us to start thinking about the real implications of media change for learning as evident in the everyday lives of people young and old. In time, I believe they will enable us to better understand the real implications of media change for the future of education. Further, I believe they can empower learners to become more self-conscious of their own relationship to a rapidly changing media environment.

Summary

This chapter conceptualizes media change in terms of a dialectical synthesis between a top-down culture industry model of education (associated with mass media) and an emergent web-based participatory culture (associated with new media) and suggests that the implications for education are profound and wide-ranging. This cultural shift has already started to destabilize institutionalized forms of educational provision and these trends seem set to continue. Indeed, an emergent tradition of educational research has started to map out and describe the ways participatory cultures support the emergence of self-directed learning activities beyond formal educational contexts. Ethnographic studies provide the deepest insights into the complex relationships between learning, motivation, identity and play. However, research focused on the practices of college students promises to provide the deepest insights into what the Internet might be like for future generations. Consequently, I argue that an investigation focused on the practices of university students may allow us to peer into the future of higher education in particular and the future of (self) education in general. The chapter concludes with a brief overview of the study I conducted to advance this line of investigation and identifies the sociocultural tradition as a resource that can help us better understand self-directed learning in participatory cultures.

2 Cognitive anthropology on the Cyberian frontier

Introduction

Sociocultural and Activity Theory finds its origins in the influential work of Lev Vygotsky, and is well suited to advancing research into emergent learning practices in a rapidly changing media environment. It offers some powerful ideas that have proved useful for understanding identity and agency in new media ecologies. Further, I believe this tradition can provide a way of investigating and thinking about the real implications of media change for learning, cognition and the future of (self) education. In what follows, the reader is given an introduction to the evolving tradition of sociocultural and activity theory. Finally, I explain why sociocultural analysis of university students' purposeful actions mediated by digital tools – what I call digitally mediated practices – can provide a grounded insight into advanced new media literacies in action.

Sociocultural and activity theory: an overview

Sociocultural and activity theory is a general term used to characterize a cross-disciplinary research agenda. As a tradition it might be conceived as a broad church with multiple factions with different priorities and commitments. The multi-disciplinary nature of the tradition makes it difficult to define. Rather, it works as an umbrella term for those committed to developing a holistic understanding of the complex relationships between mind, culture and activity. Jim Wertsch *et al.* (1995) argue that the aim of sociocultural research is to 'explicate the relationship between human actions, on the one hand, and the cultural, institutional, and historical situations in which it occurs, on the other' (p. 11). In general it offers a set of concepts and methodological directives for investigating emergent developmental processes over time.

All theorists working within this tradition acknowledge the influence of Lev Vygotsky and his followers Alexandre Luria and Alexei Leont'ev who become known as the Soviet school of cultural-historical psychology. Ideas emerging from this tradition have been seeping into the Western academy since the translation and publication of Vygotsky's *Thought and Language* in 1962. Today, traditions of research inspired by the work of Vygotsky and his followers have attracted the interest of psychologists, anthropologists, sociologists, media theorists, computer-human interaction researchers and management scientists as well as educationalists. In turn, ideas emerging from theses traditions have often been used to refine, challenge and develop concepts emerging more directly from the Soviet school.

The cross-fertilization of ideas across disciplines has helped to nurture a rich, generative and evolving debate that transcends disciplinary boundaries. For example, in the American Academy leading sociocultural theorists Jim Wertsch (1991, 1998) has synthesized Vygotsky with the work of Mikhail Bakhtin (1981) and the symbolic interactionism of Kenneth Burke (1969). Likewise, Michael Cole (1996), who was involved in the early translations of Vygotsky's work and describes himself as a 'Cultural Psychologist' has highlighted parallels between the thought of American pragmatists (Austin *et al.* 1978; Dewey 1998) and sociocultural theorists. Similarly, in Europe, Yrjö Engeström, the leading proponent of activity theoretical research, is indebted to the pioneering work of the cognitive anthropologist Gregory Bateson (2000).

This book explores the utility of the sociocultural theory for understanding the implications of media change for learning, cognition and education. The sociocultural tradition remains foundational. However, each chapter borrows and synthesizes concepts emerging from other traditions. To this end, ideas emerging from the new literacy movement (Gee 1996, 2000a; New London Group 2000; Street 1984), theories of digital, techno or new media literacy (Jenkins *et al.* 2006; Lankshear and Knobel 2003; Snyder 1998), multimodality theory (Kress 2000, 2003), cognitive science (Clark 2003; Dennett 1996), cyber-economics (Battelle 2006; Castronova 2001; Goldhaber 1997) and game theory (Gee 2003; Shaffer 2005) have proved useful as sensitizing concepts. Chapters 3 through 7 use ideas from these traditions to guide and focus the work of conceptual development. This chapter remains focused on the central tenets of the sociocultural tradition. It identifies contemporary innovations in the tradition which can help us understand emergent learning practices associated with digital media. Further, it explains why a sociocultural approach can help us develop a grounded insight in what we mean by new media literacy.

The central tenets of sociocultural research

In his seminal work, Michael Cole (1996: 104) summarizes the central tenets of the tradition as a seven point schema.

- It emphasizes mediated action in a context.
- It insists on the importance of the "genetic method", understood broadly to include historical, ontogenetic and microgenetic levels of analysis.

- It seeks to ground analysis in everyday life events.
- It assumes that mind emerges in the joint mediated activity of people. Mind, then, is in an important sense, 'co-constructed' and distributed.
- It assumes that individuals are active agents in their own development but do not act in settings of their own choosing.
- It rejects cause-effect, stimulus-response, explanatory science in favor of a science that emphasizes the emergent nature of mind in activity and that acknowledges a central role for interpretation in its explanatory framework.
- It draws upon methodologies from the humanities as well as from the social and biological sciences.

These tenets provide a general orientation and inform the approach adopted in this book. The following sections elaborate in order to illustrate their relevance for understanding the implications of media change for learning.[1]

Vygotsky's genetic method

Vygotsky and his followers developed a method known as the 'genetic method' (Wertsch 1985: 17–57). The method has been used to understand developmental processes at multiple levels of analysis. Most commonly, the genetic method is used to understand how humans use tools and resources to solve problems in real time. Studies of this kind work at a microgenetic level of analysis. Such an approach has been used by sociocultural researchers to study dairy pre-loaders (Scribner 1988), ski instruction (Burton and Brown 1988), grocery shopping (Lave *et al.* 1984), and interactions between toddlers and care-givers (Rogoff *et al.* 1993). The genetic method might also be used in an attempt to understand ontogeny, or the development of an organism or a person over a lifetime (Valsiner 1997). In Chapter 6 an extended vignette that attempts to illustrate how a variety of cultural tools mediated an individual's lifelong learning agenda works at the ontogenetic level of analysis. Finally, the genetic method draws on documentary evidence or the findings of previous research to conceptualize cultural-historical processes over time. The section entitled, 'from the culture industry to participatory culture,' in Chapter 1, works at this level of analysis. Viewed holistically, this book is an attempt to understand the intersection between media change (cultural-historical development), the emergent learning practices of individuals (microgenesis) and personal development over a lifetime (ontogeny).

Mediation through the use of cultural tools

In the sociocultural tradition the term 'tool' denotes any kind of cultural artefact that humans have invented to expand physical or cognitive capabilities. As a species, humans have invented and used tools from clubs and hammers to musical notation systems and language systems to work, create, communicate and solve problems. From this perspective, digital tools such as spreadsheets, blogs and wikis are just the latest additions to the available cultural toolkit.

The concept of *mediation* helps us to understand how intentional actions shape and are shaped by the use of tools in purposeful activity. It has become a foundational concept in the sociocultural tradition. Indeed, before his untimely death at the age of thirty-seven, Vygotsky himself proposed that 'the central fact about psychology is the fact of mediation' (cited in Cole and Wertsch 1996: 251). It has since become a foundational concept for an integrated science of understanding human actions, thought and behaviour.

In order to understand the mediational properties of tools it is essential to understand how people actually use tools to serve their purposes. Wertsch (1985) stresses:

> Whilst cultural tools or artefacts involved in mediation certainly play an essential role in *shaping* action, they do not *determine* or *cause* action in some kind of static, mechanistic way. Indeed, in and of themselves, cultural tools are powerless to do anything. They can have their impact only when individuals *use* them.
>
> (Wertsch 1985: 22)

He continues:

> The point of all this is to remind us that the study of mediation and mediated action cannot focus solely on the cultural tools involved. Even the most sophisticated analysis of these tools cannot itself tell us how they are taken up and used by individuals to carry out action.
>
> (Ibid.)

These ruminations sensitize us to the futility of studying web-based tools and resources in themselves. They direct sociocultural researchers to study how learners discover, tinker and put digital tools to use in everyday life.

In order to study tool-mediated actions it is important to understand how tools both *constrain* and *afford* thought and action. For example, Twitter, a relatively new addition to our cultural toolkit, *affords* users the possibility of microblogging short messages to a globally distributed personal network. However, messages sent on Twitter are restricted by a 140 character limit. Thus, predesigned features of the tool *constrain* the kinds of communicative practices it affords. Nevertheless, in everyday life people use Twitter in variety of different ways to serve their purposes. Consequently, only by examining the practices of an individual as they put Twitter to use for specific purposes can we start to understand how the tool pushes back and shapes the actions and intentions of the user. In turn the researcher is able to develop a fuller understanding of microblogging conceived as an emergent form of communicative practice.

This dialectical mode of thinking about mediation informs the analysis of students' use of digital tools throughout this book.

The method of double stimulation

Vygotsky and his followers developed the method of 'double stimulation' in an attempt to study instances of developmental growth in children's problem solving activity. It encourages us to investigate tool-mediated actions at a microgenetic level of analysis. Vygotsky's description of the method is worth quoting at length:

> Our approach to the study of these processes is to use what we call the functional *method of double stimulation*. The task facing the child in the experimental context is, as a rule, beyond his present capabilities and cannot be solved by existing skills. In such cases a neutral object is placed near the child, and frequently we are able to observe how the neutral stimulus is drawn into the situation and takes on the function of a sign. Thus, the child actively incorporates these neutral objects into the task of problem solving [...], In this way, we are able to study the *process of accomplishing a task by the aid of specific auxiliary means*.
>
> (Vygotsky 1978: 4)

Critically, stimulation is not directly applied. Rather, the researchers simply place a tool within the child's reach and observe how they appropriate or use the tool to accomplish the task. Using this method, Vygotsky was able to explore how and why learners adopt and start to use tools to achieve their purposes. Significantly, this method ensures that inferences about the learning processes involved are always grounded in concrete observation of practice. The hypotheses that arise might be disputed, refined or rejected. Nevertheless, the approach ensures that the theory generated is always grounded in the concrete analysis of tool-mediated actions.

The method I developed as a doctoral student to study the practices of learners mediated by digital tools was inspired, in part, by this method. However, I was more interested in understanding how university students were creatively appropriating digital tools and resources that they had access to through the Internet to solve problems, expand learning opportunities and address authentic learning needs.

Agency and mediation

In order to understand human agency it is essential to understand how humans use a variety of tools to mediate (or regulate) their own actions, purposes and intentions. Vygotsky continually stresses that individuals master their own behaviour through the use of external stimuli:

As I have repeatedly emphasized, an essential mechanism of the reconstructive process that takes place during a child's development is the creation and use of a number of artificial stimuli. These play an auxiliary role that permits human beings to master their own behaviour, at first by external means and later by more complex inner operations.

(Vygotsky 1978: 73)

As the quotation suggests, with time the use of the new tool starts to function as an internalized psychological tool, mediating thought and action, even when the original stimuli are no longer present. Once internalized, these psychological tools become powerful yet invisible mediators that assist individuals in achieving mastery and self-control.

Vygotsky (1986) himself was interested in the mediational properties of spoken language. Indeed, he regarded speech (spoken and internalized) as the 'tool of tools' that structured thought and action from the inside. For example, children often talk to themselves as they attempt to solve problems in an attempt to regulate their own purposeful actions and stay focused on a particular task. Adults more typically use inner (or unspoken) speech to self-regulate intentional actions especially when working on difficult or challenging tasks. Nevertheless, from a sociocultural perspective language is just one (albeit important) cultural tool that can be used to regulate goal-directed actions.

Researchers interested in child development have studied how carers, tutors and peers mediate the intentional actions of infants (Forman and Cazden 1985; Resnick 1996; Rogoff 1990, 2003). Researchers interested in higher order thinking have investigated mediation via external representations or models such as to-do lists, diagrams and flow charts (Norman 1993; Wartofsky 1979; Kozulin 2003). Others have explored how the structural properties of particular environments mediate collective activities over time (González *et al.* 2004; Moll *et al.* 1992; Valsiner 1997). With the rise of the information technology revolution researchers became more interested in the mediational properties of electronic instrumentation and information and communication technologies (Hutchins 1995b, 1997; Ludvigsen *et al.* 2007; Norman 1993, 2002; Pea 1985; Säljö 1999). At the same time, researchers have started to explore how internalized narratives, scripts and self-schemas mediate intentional actions, thought and behaviour (Bruner 1986, 1991; Wertsch 1998, 2002).

This book is primarily concerned with understanding how students use digital tools to take control and mediate their own purposes as learners. However, no form of mediation is excluded if it helps us understand the implications of media change for learning. Indeed, in this book learners' identities, or more precisely learners' 'projective identities' (Gee 2003) or imagined future selves are conceived of as invisible but powerful mediators of self-directed learning activity.

Finding a unit of analysis that illuminates the whole

Historically, finding a unit of analysis that allowed researchers to escape dualistic assumptions about the relationship between mind, culture and activity posed considerable challenges (Davydov and Radzikhovskii 1985; Zinchenko 1985). From a sociocultural perspective, developmental processes cannot be viewed independently of the socio-historical context. Consequently, the interrelationships between microgenetic, ontogenetic and cultural-historical levels of analysis must be revealed by the unit of analysis selected. Vygotsky regarded the separation of psychological processes from the cultural toolkit that mediates psychological processes as a fundamental error. To emphasize this point he used an analogy. He noted that if someone interested in why water extinguishes fire divided the water molecule into its constituent elements they would be surprised to find out that hydrogen burns and oxygen sustains fire. The analogy illustrates that reductive analysis invariably fails to explain the properties of the whole (Wertsch 1985: 194). Indeed, for the Soviet school both Pavlov's behaviourism on the one hand and idealistic Gestalt psychology on the other remained trapped within a dualistic concept of mind. They argued that a method was required that help us understand cognitive processes as a situated, embodied and distributed phenomena mediated by cultural tools. As Michael Cole (1985: 279–390) has stressed, both failed to take account of the ways 'culture and cognition create each other'.

Contemporary sociocultural researchers have accepted tool-mediated actions as the central unit of analysis. Developmental processes are studied through a detailed analysis of tool-mediated actions as they evolve over time. This approach does not separate psychological processes from the available cultural toolkit. Further, it encourages the research to understand how tools mediate human thought and action.

As things become more complicated, it is necessary to understand how hundreds of tool-mediated actions are co-ordinated to work on more complex objects. To this end, activity theorists study more object-orientated activities (Engeström 1987; Engeström *et al.* 1999). For example, hundreds of operations (mediated by a variety of different digital tools and resources) might be employed to produce a written assignment (the object-motive of the activity). This object-orientated activity also involves a *division of labour* (e.g. planning, drafting, editing, proofing, etc.), is constrained by various *rules* (e.g. a word limit) and may involve input and feedback from others (i.e. tutors and course mates) that might be regarded as the *community*. The object (in this case the written assignment) motivates the task and demands the selection of particular tools and adherence to rules or procedures. For this reason, the object and motive of the activity system are conceived as an indivisible whole called the object-motive. Indeed, activity theorists often refer to the object-motive as that which is worked upon and simultaneously bites back and defines the structural dynamics of the activity. In this respect, microgenetic analysis of individual tool-mediated actions should never be considered independently of the wider activity system.

In general, sociocultural researchers analyse tool-mediated actions in order to understand developmental processes as they evolve over time. A central challenge is to understand the system holistically through an analysis of specific tool-mediated actions. In the introduction to Vygotsky's *Mind in Society* (1978), Cole and Scribner note that his approach parallels the method employed by Marx to investigate socio-economic phenomena:

> The whole of *Capital* is written according to the following method: Marx analyses a single living 'cell' of capitalist society – for example, the nature of value. Within this cell he discovers the structure of the entire system and all of its economic institutions.
>
> (Cole and Scribner 1978: 8, italics in original)

They add, 'to the layman this analysis may seem a murky tangle of tiny details', but stress that these tiny details are 'exactly those' which are essential to the 'microanatomy' of the whole (ibid.). Similarly, sociocultural researchers have tended to accept 'tool-mediated-action' (Wertsch 1985, 1998) as the primary unit of analysis and the 'microcosm' that illuminates the structure of the whole. Throughout this book microgenetic analysis of purposive actions mediated by digital tools and resources provide the microcosm that illuminates the whole and leads me to propose that as a result of media change we may be witnessing the decentring of the traditional university. The theory may be disputed and hypotheses that arise may be questioned, modified or rejected. Nevertheless, the concrete observations (presented throughout this book as a series of richly descriptive vignettes) anchor the work of conceptual development.

In practice, students' use of digital tools was investigated through observation (or stimulated response) and indirectly through interview and retrospective virtual ethnography. The Appendix provides a more detailed account of the methodological procedure employed during data collection.

Learning in a zone of proximal development

All tools are invented by humans. Consequently, in the process of learning to use tools learners internalize the knowledge and expertise of the tool makers. In this respect tools are imbued with our cultural legacies and allow each generation to benefit from the knowledge and expertise of previous generations that has become designed into the available cultural toolkit. Thus, unlike primates, human beings have the potential to start from where the previous generation left off. Indeed, from a sociocultural perspective it is our capacity to use tools that has allowed human beings to pull away from animals in philogenesis (or evolutionary time) and develop higher psychological functions.

Learning is evident in the increasingly developed use of tools to achieve our purposes (Säljö 1999). For example, learning might involve the process of learning to use spoken words to ask for food, learning to use an abstract concept to solve a mathematical problem or learning to use a social book-marking tool to share links to interesting websites. Further through continued use we start to internalize psychological tools, like mathematical formulae. Once internalized these psychological tools start to mediate thought and action from the inside – even when the original tool is no longer present. Nevertheless, many tools, like word processors and spreadsheets, can never be fully internalized. In these cases, the cognitive load required for accomplishing a task is distributed between the intelligence designed into the tool and the intelligence of the tool user (Pea 1997).

The 'zone of proximal development' (ZPD) has become a foundational concept within the sociocultural tradition for investigating and thinking about learning as the use of tools. In general, the concept of the ZPD shifts attention away from thinking about learning as an individual activity. Rather, it encourages us to explore what learners are capable of achieving with the aid of tools, props or under the guidance of a more experienced tutor (Rogoff and Wertsch 1984; Wood *et al.* 1976). Vygotsky defines the ZPD as 'the distance between a child's actual developmental level as determined through independent problem solving and [his or her] potential development [level] as determined through problem solving under adult guidance or a collaboration with more capable peers' (Vygotsky 1978: 86). Within the ZPD, the cognitive load required to perform a task or solve a problem is effectively shared or distributed between the learner and the tutor.

In the digital age, the cognitive load required to perform many everyday tasks is distributed between learners and digital tools such as spreadsheets, electronic organizers and search engines that are designed to enhance and expand our information processing capabilities. In these cases it becomes more appropriate to talk about what Perkins (1997) describes as learning in person-plus mode. Moreover, many digital applications now embed intelligent agents that are specifically designed to support and guide users as they learn to use the application. In these cases, learners are still benefiting from the knowledge and expertise of others that is now implicit in the design of the tool.

In the West, educational researchers have tended to explore how educators might 'scaffold' (Pea 2004; Wood *et al.* 1976) student learning to position them in a zone of proximal development. For example, teachers typically provide less able students with writing templates that simplify the task. The level of scaffolding is then faded, or progressively withdrawn until a child can perform unassisted. In this process, the locus of control remains with the teacher. Vygotsky himself was more interested in how learners actively appropriated new tools and leveraged the assistance of more experienced practitioners to position themselves within a ZPD. This line of thought has been more fully developed in Engeström's theory of 'expansive learning' (1987, 2001) and Edwards' (2005; Edwards and D'Arcy 2004) work on 'relational agency'. Both theorists foreground the creative potential of humans as active agents capable of transforming the conditions of action and seeking out others as a resource to work on shared objects. Indeed these ideas encourage us to see learners as active agents in their own development capable of transforming the context of action and positioning themselves within a ZPD. This book develops this trajectory of theoretical inquiry. It reveals how advanced learners are creatively appropriating a burgeoning variety of digital tools as study aids, cultivating globally distributed funds of living knowledge and generating virtually figured worlds that positioning them in zones of proximal development and turbo boost personal agency. In short, it explores how learners are transforming the quasi-virtual contexts of their own learning and personal development.

Cognitive anthropology and studies of cognition in the wild

This book offers new categories for understanding emergent learning practices in an emerging media landscape. However, the work of conceptual development is grounded in an ethnographic investigation that involved periods of observation, in-depth interviews and short periods of virtual ethnography following a sustained period of immersion in the field. In this respect, the approach adopted follows the tradition established by cognitive anthropologists.

Historically, cognitive anthropologists have stressed the importance of studying 'everyday cognition' (Rogoff and Lave 1984) or 'cognition in the wild' (Hutchins 1995a, 1995b) in real world situated contexts. As a result, contemporary cognitive anthropology and socio-cultural research has converged into an overlapping field of inquiry. Today cognitive anthropologists such as Gregory Bateson (2000) and Edwin Hutchins (1995a, 1995b) are widely cited in the work of those who identify themselves as sociocultural and activity theorists. At the same time cognitive anthropologists such as Barbara Rogoff (1990) and Dorothy Holland *et al.* (1998) use Vygotskian concepts to analyse data sets produced by ethnographic field work. However, unlike researchers coming into the field of sociocultural research with a training in psychology or linguistics, cognitive anthropologists tend to immerse themselves in the field for a sustained period of time and make extensive use of rich description in their analysis. In this respect the influence of cultural anthropology and the ethnographic tradition is more conspicuous in the work of cognitive anthropologists. However, the aim is to develop new concepts that can be used to understand psychological processes more generally. In this study, the aim is to develop new concepts, grounded in detailed analysis of students' everyday use of digital tools, that can be used to understand emergent learning practices in new mediascapes more generally. It is hoped that these concepts will guide further research and help readers understand how they might make more effective use of the Internet as a learning resource.

The specific conceptual building blocks used as heuristics to identify and explore each genre of learning activity are introduced at the start of each chapter. However, to orientate the reader, the following three sections provides an overview of contemporary developments that I regard as foundational to the trajectory of theoretical innovation that I develop throughout this book. The first section foregrounds the importance of Engeström's (1987) notion of expansive learning. The second foregrounds the utility of conceptual work by James Paul Gee (2003, 2004) and Dorothy Holland *et al.* (1998) for understanding the importance of identity conceived as a mediator and motivator of informal learning activity. The third section explains why I believe a sociocultural approach can advance our understanding of what it means to be literate in an emergent media landscape.

Expansive learning: double binds, breaking away and horizontal developments

The bulk of existing work within the sociocultural tradition explores how learners internalize knowledge and become progressively enculturated into existing forms of social practice. This is particularly conspicuous in the 'communities of practice' model (Lave and Wenger 1991; Wenger 1998) in which apprentices progressively imitate and later reproduce the practices of the masters. These theorists have helped us understand how institutionalized practices become reified and are reproduced over time. In this respect, there are strong parallels with French microsociology (Bourdieu 1977) and Giddens' (1984) structuration theory. However, these studies rarely draw attention to the capacity for individuals and collectives to take on active roles in transforming the conditions of their own development. Indeed, for those interested in transformation and change, Lave and Wenger's communities of practice model appears inherently conservative. Further, this model tends to assume that enculturation is a smooth, progressive and gradual process. The tensions, upheavals and contradictions that characterize many developmental processes are often lost. In contrast, for Vygotsky and his followers, the resourcefulness and creative potential of humans is invariably revealed in critical moments when learners cannot proceed without assistance and consciously seek out tools, resources and the assistance of others in order to proceed.

In Engeström's (1987) theory of expansive learning, the tensions, contradictions and sudden transformations that characterize the development process are more conspicuous. Indeed, the notion of expansive learning highlights the way individuals and groups 'break away' from traditional institutionalized practices and set about transforming the contexts of their own learning and development. According to Engeström (1996), this theory of development moves beyond models proposed by either Vygotsky or Piaget:

> Recent work based on dialectics and the cultural-historical theory of activity points towards three major challenges to the development

of both Vygotsky and Piaget: (1) instead of just benign achievement of mastery, development may be viewed as partially destructive rejection of the old; (2) instead of just individual transformation, development may be viewed as collective transformation; (3) instead of just vertical movement across levels, development may be viewed as horizontal movement across borders.

(Engeström 1996: 126)

The emphasis on 'destructive rejection of the old', 'collective transformations' and 'horizontal developments across borders' seems particularly relevant for understanding how learners are exploiting access to the Internet to transform the conditions of their own learning and personal development. For example, it draws attention to the ways learners are breaking away from the traditional modes of learning and instruction, it encourages us to understand how learners are exploiting access to the Internet to expand learning opportunities and it encourages us to understand how new media empower individuals and groups to make horizontal developments that transcend institutional boundaries.

Expansive learning theory also draws attention to ways learners, caught up in a rapidly changing media environment, can become more conscious of their own predicament. This movement towards self-consciousness as a prequel to an expansive transformation finds its origins in the work of Ilyenkov, the philosophical mentor of Vygotsky and the Soviet school. He stressed:

Consciousness only arises where the individual is compelled to look at himself as if from the side — as if with the eyes of another person, the eyes of all other people — only where he is compelled to correlate his individual actions with the actions of another man, that is to say, only within the framework of collectively performed life activity.

(Ilyenkov 1977: 24)

Following Ilyenkov, Engeström's work suggests that learners must become aware of the tensions and contradictions retarding their own development prior to initiating and expansive transformation. This is achieved when an individual or a group gains an alternative perspective as though looking at themselves through the eyes of another.

This provides a very different model to that implied in Wenger's (1998) idea of a community of practice where the apprentice becomes progressively enculturated (possibly unconsciously) into a pre-existing way of knowing, doing and interacting with the environment. It stresses the need for students to become more conscious of ways a particular configuration of resources mediates their own action, thought and behaviour. Further, it highlights the need to make students more conscious of the tensions and contradictions in their personalized cognitive ecologies that may be retarding development.

Indeed, a heightened state of self-consciousness (often associated with a period of frustration, discontentment or stress) often precedes an expansive transformation in which people consciously set about transforming the conditions of their own learning and personal development.

To clarify, it is helpful to consider the origins of Engeström's (1987) theory of expansive learning in the highly original work of cognitive anthropologist Gregory Bateson. Bateson (1978) proposed three types of learning:

Learning I is associated with stimulus-response behavioural psychology and refers to the conditioning and acquisition of the responses deemed correct in a given context – for instance, the learning of correct answers in a classroom.

Learning II (or deep learning) occurs when people acquire the deep-seated rules and patterns of behaviour characteristic to the context itself. This model appears implicit in work that discusses progressive enculturation into communities of practice (Wenger 1998) and guided participation (Rogoff *et al.* 1993) in which individuals gradually master the practices of experts and tutors. However, as a result of a slave-like adherence to traditional practices, learners sometimes find themselves caught in a 'double bind'. In these situations, no matter what subjects do, they cannot achieve their goals.

Learning III occurs when a person or a group begins to radically question the sense and meaning of the context and reconstructs a wider alternative context. In effect, Learning III precedes an expansive transformation. At this point learners start to 'break away' and actively seek out new tools, resources and other people in an attempt to transform the context of their own learning and development. Alternatively, if this is not possible, they might make a 'horizontal development' into an alternative context that allows them to grow and develop among a new ecology of resources.

This book is concerned with Learning III. It focuses attention on the way learners are seeking out new tools and resources (including human resources) to transform the quasi-virtual contexts of their own learning and personal development. In general, expansive learning theory offers some powerful tools for understanding the predicament of learners caught up in a period of rapid media change at both an individual and systemic level. Nevertheless, it is not sufficient for our purposes. For example, expansive learning does not take account of some of the more subtle ways learners identities are shaped by and shape their own practices. Nevertheless, recent work has opened a door to a sociocultural mode of thinking about identity as a mediator and motivator of learning activity that can help us better understand student learning in participatory cultures.

Dorothy Holland *et al.*'s (1998) influential work on *Identity and Agency in Cultural Worlds* and James Paul Gee's (2004) more recent work that investigates the experience of virtual role-play in immersive game worlds have proved particularly useful. They have both helped me understand how learner identities are formed and subsequently shape their participation in virtual ecologies. To these theorists I now turn.

Projective identities and virtually figured worlds

Gee's (2003, 2004) work draws attention to the way learners might work at becoming an imagined future self or 'projective identity.' The concept emerges from his studies of situated learning and language acquisition in the context of video game play. He argues that virtual role-play involves an interplay between a player's real-world identity (that which a player brings with them to a role), a virtual identity (that which a player develops through the choices they make) and a projective identity (the quasi-virtual self that the player is aiming to become). This concept is illustrated with reference to the experience of playing a female Half Elf in the video game Arcanium:

> A game like *Arcanium* allows me, the player, certain degrees of freedom (choices) in forming my virtual character and developing her throughout the game. In my projective identity I worry about what sorts of 'person' I want her to be, and what type of history I want her to have had by the time I am done. I want this person and history to reflect my values – though I have to think reflectively and critically about these, since I have never had to project a Half Elf onto the world before. At the same time, this person and history I am building also reflects what I have learned from playing the game and being Bead in the land of *Arcanium*.
> (Gee 2004: 112)

Indeed, the three-way play of real world, virtual world and projective identity is regarded as a powerful experience that might support learning through designed experiences in immersive game worlds. This leads one to conceive of immersive game worlds as incubators that afford learners opportunities to acquire knowledge and skills as they work towards the actualization of a projective identity.

Gee's work is highly suggestive. Nevertheless, immersive game worlds are not the only virtually environments that afford new opportunities for identity work. Any virtual ecology might provide an alternative context for identity work. Indeed, this way of thinking has proved useful for understanding how learners, like Isaac and Heather, shape their virtually figured worlds that then thereafter shape their identities and the sense of who they might become. The work of Holland *et al.* (1998) provides a set of categories that help us think about identity formation in a variety of cultural constructed or figured worlds.

In the work of Holland *et al.* (1998) 'figured worlds' are conceived of as holistic mediators of human action, behaviour and development. They do not exist independently of human activity. Rather, they exist as the product of human activity. Holland *et al.* (1998) stress that all varieties of human activity give rise to figured worlds:

> Under the rubric of culturally figured worlds or figured worlds we include all those cultural realms peopled by characters from collective imaginings: academia, the factory, crime, romance, environmental activism, games of Dungeons and Dragons, the men's house among the Mehinaku of Brazil (Gregor 1977). These are worlds made up of Geertz's (1973b) 'webs of meaning.' Figured worlds take shape within and grant shape to the co-production of activities, discourses, performances, and artefacts.
>
> (Holland *et al.* 1998: 51)

Importantly, figured worlds are not simply products of the imagination but come into being and are sustained through the mediated practices of those who actively participate in them. For example, the figured world of Roman Catholicism is populated by priests and congregations. It is mediated by a variety of religious artefacts such as churches, prayer books and crucifixes, and exists as the amalgam of ritualistic practices mediated by these tools such as the Morning Prayer or the singing of hymns. From this perspective Roman Catholicism is a culturally constructed figured world consisting of religious artefacts, rituals and discursive practices that mediate the intentional states and actions of participants. Holland *et al.* (1998) stress that figured worlds are 'peopled by the figures, characters, and types who carry out its tasks and who also have styles of interacting within, distinguishable perspectives on, and orientations toward it' (p. 51). Thus in certain respects participants are subjugated by the figured worlds in which they participate and tend to assume the subject positions that are foisted upon them. Nevertheless, humans have agency and the capacity to resist these subject positions. Indeed, in this framework, identities are not innate or fixed. This process of resistance typically involves drawing upon other voices, memories and practiced identities outside of the current context of action. Furthermore, figured worlds are the product of collective human activity, therefore individuals and groups have it within their power to transform the figured worlds that position them as subjects. Indeed, through dialogue and collective action, people can create alternative contexts that allow them to transform their sense of who they are and who they might become. This transformative practice is described as 'making worlds' (Holland *et al.* 1998: 235–252).

In Chapter 6, I conceive of students' personalized media environments as a species of figured world, or more precisely what I call *virtually figured worlds*. A central challenge is to better understand how learners design and shape their virtually figured world, and how, in turn, these virtually figured worlds shape a learner's sense of who they are and who they might become. Holland *et al.*'s (1998) work is useful in this respect because it helps us understand how entrance into a figured world starts to shape a participant's identity. They argue: 'people's identities and agency are formed dialectically and dialogically in these as if worlds.' And add: 'people have the propensity to be drawn to, recruited for, and formed in these worlds, and to become active in and passionate about them.' (p. 50). Over time these practiced identities are internalized as 'history in person' and continue to mediate a subject's action and behaviour from the inside even when they move across contexts.

I believe this mode of thinking is fruitful for understanding how virtually figured worlds start to shape students' sense of who they are and who they might become. For example, this way of thinking can help us understand how the Warhammer gaming community, conceived as a virtually figured world, shaped Isaac's emerging sense of self as he became passionate about the new identity of the 'Warhammer 40K Celebrity' he took on (Tobin 1998). Likewise, it appears useful for thinking about the way *The Daily Prophet*, conceived as a virtually figured world, mediated Heather's development as a teen editor as she started to take on adult roles and responsibilities (Jenkins 2006c). In both cases virtually figured worlds mediate the process of self-formation and start to reinforce Heather and Isaac's commitment to a particular projective identity or imagined future self. In Chapter 6 I elaborate on this argument in an attempt to understand how advanced agentive students work on their projective identities through a form of serious play within quasi-virtual ecologies of their own figuration.

Digitally mediated practice as new media literacy

This final section explains why a sociocultural approach can help us develop a more robust, grounded and analytical concept of new media literacy. This is necessary to advance a field of inquiry that has become so central to the field of digital media and learning. To date, much has been written on the topic. However, few have advanced an empirical method for advancing this field of inquiry.

From the late 1990s onwards, scholars started to write about 'techno', 'silicon' or 'digital' literacies (Gilster 1997; Tyner 1998; Kress 2003; Kist 2005; Lankshear and Knobel 2003; Durrant and Beavis 2004; Snyder 1998, 2002). The sentiment driving this movement is well captured in a quotation from Kress who argues:

> It is no longer possible to think about literacy in isolation from a vast array of social, technological and economic factors. Two distinct yet

related factors deserve to be particularly highlighted. These are, on the one hand, the broad move from the now centuries old long dominance of writing to the new dominance of the image and, on the other hand, the move from the dominance of the medium of the book to the dominance of the medium of the screen.

(Kress 2003: 20)

Traditionally, many writers who have contributed to this field have a background in the humanities and teach on English or communication studies courses. It is perhaps a flair for writing and sensitivity to detailed textual analysis that make these essays such a thrilling read. Two influential volumes, *Page to Screen: Taking Literacy into the Electronic Era* (1998) and *Silicon Literacies: Communication, Innovation and Education in the Electronic Age* (2002), both collected and edited by Illana Snyder, convey the breadth and richness of the field. Stylistically these essays betray the influence of cultural studies traditions. The authors write elegantly, working at a high level of abstraction, often traversing a range of issues within a single article whilst referencing a disparate array of theorists. Indeed, the focus of interest shifts rapidly within and between volumes from reviews of existing studies on written composition with word processors (Hawisher and Selfe 1998) to articles on *The rhetorics and Languages of Electronic Mail* (Moran and Hawisher 1998), hypermedia navigation and *The Wired World of Second Language Acquisition* (Knobel *et al.* 1998). Later Abbot (2002) investigated the use of 'emoticons' in instant relay chat and Joyce (1998) explored non-linear hypertext narratives. Concepts pillaged from diverse humanistic traditions are used to theorize literacy in the electronic era. According to Snyder (2002: xxv), 'what emerges is a recognition that research in this area has begun the important process of careful and critical borrowing.' Nevertheless, no coherent method is advocated for advancing the study of new media literacies and no coherent theoretical framework is offered that might help work within this field connect and build cumulatively on existing work in the learning sciences. Indeed, many writers in this tradition simply make inferences from an analysis of screen-based texts.

Colin Lankshear and Michele Knobel (2003) are among a handful of new literacy theorists who study the *practices* of young people as they use digital tools and resources and then abstract beyond the particularities of each case. Further, their analysis draws attention to the creativity and ingenuity of learners as they appropriate new media to advance their purposes beyond the confines of formal educational contexts. Microgenetic analysis draws attention to a variety of digital subcultural practices such as 'multimediating', 'e-zining', 'memeing' and 'culture jamming' (op. cit.: 33–49) that allow young people to develop a rich repertoire of new media literacies. Further, their work moves beyond the descriptive level and offers categories that challenge common sense assumptions about the educational potential of the

Internet. In this respect, their work provides a model and source of inspiration for this book. For example, Lankshear and Knobel are highly critical of the National Grid for Learning; a multimillion pound government sponsored initiative that promised to provide schools with a rich depository of progressive online interactive resources (op. cit.: 81–107). They regard the high level of constraints and regulations that allow teachers to control access and use to be emblematic of an 'outside mindset' and argue that sites of this type provide young people with 'unfortunate experiences' of using the Internet that may offend their 'insider sensitivities' and risk turning them off (op. cit.: 104). In contrast, eBay.com is presented as an example of an online space that enculturates its users into an 'insider mindset'. Indeed, the authors claim that 'eBay teaches people how they should act within the new cyberspace' and go so far as to claim that eBay 'socializes people about what counts as an exemplary global space, encouraging the right kind of cyber practices that lead to a well-organised and civil World Wide Web' (op. cit.: 138).

Jenkins *et al.* (2006) have also developed a model for understanding new media literacy defined as the social skills and cultural competences required to become full participants in an emerging media landscape. They included: Play, Performance, Simulation, Appropriation, Multitasking, Distributed Cognition, Collective Intelligence, Judgement and Transmedia Navigation. The authors argue that 'schools and afterschool programs must devote more attention to fostering what we call the new media literacies' (p. 4) that are developed informally through collaboration and networking in participatory cultures. However, the authors stress that these skills build on the foundation of traditional literacy, research skills, technical skills, and critical analysis skills taught in the classroom. The paper speaks to a wide audience. In particular it aims to empower educational professionals to think about ways they might promote new media literacies in the classroom. In many respects the categories and typologies offered provide a powerful starting point for thinking about emergent practices associated with new media forms. Nevertheless, the paper does not offer an empirical methodology that could be used to refine and develop the study of new media literacies or explore how they are acquired and deployed in everyday life. Indeed, category development is grounded and illustrated with examples provided by existing case studies of progressive media literacies initiatives. As a result, there is a slight tendency to draw on somewhat exotic, rather than everyday examples, and celebrate the new over the old. Finally, little attention is paid to the challenges and choices confronting individuals as they attempt to engage with participatory cultures.

In this book, new media literacy is conceived of as a capacity to make effective use of digital tools and resources to address authentic needs. These might be associated with everyday practices such as e-mailing, or searching for video podcasts on YouTube or more specialist practices like constructing an online identity. No preference is given to practices associated with specific tools or technologies. Rather, the new media literacies identified are manifest in the practices of individual learners as they appropriate and put digital tools and resources to use in everyday life. The aim is to provide a more robust and grounded insight into a range of new media literacies (conceived of as expert-like practices) in action. In many respects it betrays a fetish for the mundane over the exotic.

This approach accords with a practice-based conception of literacy that has been influential since Scribner and Cole's (1981) seminal study *The Psychology of Literacy*. Commenting on this work, Olson argues:

> Literacy is not just a basic set of skills isolated from everything else. It is the competence to exploit a particular set of cultural resources. It is the evolution of those resources in conjunction with the knowledge and skill to exploit those resources for particular purposes that makes up literacy.
>
> (Olson 1994: 43)

In effect, this expands the unit of analysis beyond simple tool-mediated actions. It shifts one into thinking about how individuals become adept at exploiting the affordances of new media to succeed in an increasingly multicultural and technology-rich world. This line of thinking was developed by the New London Group (1996, 2000), a group of scholars from diverse disciplinary backgrounds,[2] who argued that we need a broader view of literacy that takes account of the multiplicity of communications channels and cultural diversity in the world today. Gee (1996) a leading figure in this group argued: 'From a sociological perspective literacy is a matter of social practices. Literacies are bound up with social, institutional and cultural relationships, and can only be understood when they are situated within their social, cultural and historical contexts' (p. xii). These insights are important for sensitizing us to the diverse ways advanced students are exploiting new media, not only to study and learn, but also to maintain connections with others from diverse social backgrounds as they move across contexts and institutional boundaries. Moreover, it draws attention to the fact that young people are growing up in a society in which individuals inhabit a plurality of lifeworlds that require them to continually adapt, negotiate and reconstruct their identity and develop new practices associated with the available cultural took kit. Failure to do so might restrict opportunities.

Summary

This chapter has introduced the reader to the central tenets of sociocultural theory as a method and theoretical toolkit for investigating emergent learning practices in new mediascapes. The chapter encourages us to understand learning as a developmental process mediated by the available (increasingly digital) cultural toolkit. It encourages us to understand how digital tools at once shape and are shaped by actions. Moreover, it encourages an understanding of how learners are positioned in and position themselves in zones of proximal development that allow them to do more than they could do unassisted. Finally, it argues that a sociocultural approach that investigates how students are using digital tools, navigating online spaces and managing their online identities can provide a grounded insight into some advanced new media literacies in action.

3   The learner as designer

Introduction

From a sociocultural perspective, when designing a particular configuration of tools and resources to support study one is effectively engaged in the process of designing an extended cognitive ecology; an ecology that regulates attention and structures physical movements and thought processes from the outside. For example, in *Things That Make Us Smart*, Norman introduces this notion with reference to a newspaper advert placed by the Wooton Patent Desk Manufacturing Company:

> The operator having arranged and classified his books, papers, etc., seats himself for business at the writing table, and realises at once that he is the master of the situation. Every portion of the desk is accessible without change of position, and all immediately before the eye. Here he discovers that perfect system and order can be attained, confusion avoided, time saved, vexations spared, dispatched in the transaction of business facilitated, and peace of mind promoted to the daily routine of business.
>
> (Norman 1993: 155)

The advert clearly implies that the desk will augment its user's information processing capabilities, lead to efficiency gains and promote 'peace of mind' as they carry out routine administrative chores. It is premised on the assumption that the cognitive load required to organize, arrange, file and retrieve multiple paper-based information sources is shared between the subject and the predesigned desktop environment.

When working with multiple digital tools on a virtual desktop the same logic applies. Tools must be made available and arranged to support the task at hand. However, within the digital domain, knowledge workers enjoy new opportunities to design, arrange and customize tools and resources to serve their changing purposes. Nevertheless, within the digital domain the learner has to assume responsibility for designing their own cognitive ecology to support advanced knowledge work. The chapter conceptualizes design, conceived as a capacity to impose control from the outside as a core new media literacy, and attempts to tease out some of the challenges and choices confronting the learner as designer.

Understanding the learner as designer

The notion that technology can expand and complement the cognitive capabilities of the human brain has been widely discussed by philosophers of cognitive science. For example, Daniel Dennett (1996) has attempted to understand the riddle of human intelligence by drawing attention to our capacity to offload cognitive chores to peripheral devices. He argues:

> The primary source, I want to suggest, is our habit of off-loading as much as possible of our cognitive tasks into the environment itself – extruding our minds (that is our mental projects and activities) into the surrounding world, where a host of peripheral devices we construct can store, process, and re-represent our meanings, streamlining, and protecting the process of transformation that are our thinking. This widespread practice of off-loading releases us from the limitations of our animal brains.
>
> (Dennett 1996: 178)

This mode of thinking highlights our capacity to 'offload' cognitive chores to external props and scaffolds that structure and regulate cognitive processes. Nevertheless, here the cognitive ecology provided by the environment is accepted as given. Further, it is unclear whether the activity of offloading is an intentional process or an unconscious 'habit'.

Philosopher Andy Clark (2003) shares Dennett's interest in the mind expanding power of technology. For Clark, human beings are *Natural-Born Cyborgs* who, since of the dawn of mankind, have invented and used technologies to expand both our physical and cognitive capabilities. Indeed, Clark's work explores the evolution of increasingly powerful cyborg minds that combine biological and non-biological components. Physical couplings between biological and non-biological elements are not required to achieve cyborgification. In many ways portable and wearable technologies, from wristwatches to mobile phones have long since extended, amplified and transformed our biological capacities. In this respect, we are and always have been what Clark describes as 'cyborgs without surgery' (p. 22). Nevertheless, as a philosopher with an interest in state of the art innovations in computer science from intelligent systems to evolutionary robotics, Clark's work tends to explore more contemporary developments in the evolution of man-machine systems. Interestingly, this tends to lead to a shift in emphasis. For example, in this passage the notion of 'offloading' is displaced by the more active and intentional notion of 'deployment'.

> We – more than any other creature on the planet – deploy non-biological elements (instruments, media, and notations) to complement our basic biological modes of processing; creating extended cognitive systems whose computational and problem solving profiles are quite different from those of the naked brain.
>
> (Clark 2003: 78)

Here, the 'deployment' trope implies greater leeway for the individual agent to actively select, deploy and strategically use particular tools, instruments and notational systems to achieve their purposes. Further, Clark's work suggests a need to adopt a systemic perspective and consider how the biological and non-biological work as components together, as part of an integrated cognitive system.

Thus, both Dennett (1996) and Clark (2003) draw attention to the various ways human beings use tools amplify, regulate and extend cognitive capacities. Nevertheless, neither writer foregrounds the work of design involved in configuring an extended cognitive system. Given our capacity to customize, personalize and design new media ecologies it seems that there is a pressing need to understand this process, and consider how design work might extend an individual's capacity to engage in advanced knowledge work.

A group of theorists known as the New London Group who were more specifically interested in learning and literacy have done more to emphasize the importance of design. In a manifesto statement the authors argue:

> The notion of design connects powerfully to the sort of creative intelligence the best practitioners need in order to be able continually to redesign their activities in the very act of practice. It connects well to the idea that learning and productivity are the results of the designs (the structures) of complex systems of people, environments, technology, beliefs, and texts.
>
> (New London Group 2000: 20)

Interestingly, this work implies that the work of design of complex systems involves the purposeful configuration of people, beliefs and texts in addition to technologies and the environment. In certain respects it sensitizes us to the fact that the design decisions we make have implications for our capacity to connect with others and experience different ways of being in the world. Further, with the focus on design, the creativity and resourcefulness of learners comes to the foreground.

Gunter Kress, a member of the New London Group who was most specifically interested in the meaning making opportunities afforded by digital and increasingly visual media, argued:

> The world of communication is now constituted in ways that make it imperative to highlight the concept of design, rather than concepts such as acquisition, or competence, or critique. This is particularly essential given new media requirements of education – even if these are not at the moment (officially) recognised.
>
> (Kress 2003: 37)

This move recognizes that meaning making practices (or semiosis) involves the recombination of multiple semiotic resources for a specific purpose.

Indeed, in Kress's theory of multimodality the concept of 'design', associated with multimodal texts like web pages (in which texts, images, icons, symbols and sound bites are combined) replaces 'writing' as the central category for understanding meaning-making practice. Kress goes so far as to claim that in the new media age 'the concept of design is the *sine qua non* of informed, reflective and productive practice' (Kress 2003: 37).[1]

In an age in which university students spend as much time reading web pages as they do reading printed pages, multimodality theory provides a powerful framework for understanding meaning-making processes. However, as a framework, multimodality theory provides limited insights into the ways learners design cognitive ecologies to enhance their capacity to engage in advanced knowledge work. This suggests a need to rethink the notion of design. This is crucial since when working with digital media, prior to making meanings, students are required to design cognitive ecologies that allow them to make particular kinds of meanings. This chapter takes up this challenge. It attempts to understand how advanced university students design new media ecologies to engage in advanced knowledge work.

The theoretical toolkit provided by the sociocultural tradition is well suited to this task. As suggested in Chapter 2, a sociocultural perspective encourages us to understand how people self-regulate intentional action from the outside. This trajectory of thought derives from Vygotsky who argued:

> The person using the power of things, or stimuli, controls his own behaviour through them, grouping them, putting them together, sorting them. In other words, the great achievement of the will consists of Man having no power over his own behaviours other than the power that things have over his behaviour.
>
> (Vygotsky 1997: 212)

In many respects, this work also draws attention to the way external stimuli shape human thought and action. However, it also emphasizes mankind's capacity to self-regulate actions and intentions from the outside through the use of external props and scaffolds. From this perspective a capacity to make effective designs is associated with increased mastery and self-control. Indeed, Vygotsky continues:

> But Man subjects to himself the power of things over behaviour, makes them serve his own purposes and controls that power as he wants. He changes his environment with the external activity and in this way affects his own behaviour, subjecting it to his own authority.
>
> (ibid.)

Reflecting upon these ideas Engeström (2005: 313) has noted, 'Vygotsky pointed out that voluntary action has two phases: a *design phase* in which the mediating artefact is painstakingly constructed and an *execution phase* which typically looks quite easy and automatic'. This chapter builds on this insight and attempts to understand the sometimes painstaking work of design that makes advanced knowledge work seemingly effortless. I begin this process with the aid of a vignette that describes how a student studying for a doctorate in psychology designed a sophisticated cognitive ecology in order to facilitate the task of brain image analysis.

Vignette: Timothy designs a cognitive ecology to support brain image analysis

Timothy, a student of clinical psychiatry, was in the final stages of producing his doctoral thesis on risk behaviour. His research involved the analysis of hundreds of MRI brain scans using specialist software.[2] Previously, he had worked in an office for graduate students at the psychiatry department where he had access to colleagues with whom he might consult. However, he now worked exclusively from his study room on a powerful desktop computer that could support dozens of applications running simultaneously. Multiple digital tools including Microsoft Word and Excel, Corel Draw and MRI-Cro (a brain image analysis package) were used in the production of the final report. All these tools were installed on the hard drive of his desktop computer. In addition, Timothy frequently consulted a specialist website (hosted by Harvard Medical School), used an online tool called the SPL Anatomy Browser, and participated in an online support group set up by the designers of the MRI-Cro brain image analysis tool. These tools and resources had become integrated into his virtual desktop and remained running in multiple windows as he worked.

Interestingly, Timothy was acutely aware of the way the design, layout and arrangement of his desktop environment impacted upon his ability to work efficiently, at an optimal level, and remain on schedule. Like many other students working on a long dissertation, he had arranged shortcuts to five folders (containing documents relating to each dissertation chapter) across his virtual desktop. He had also placed links to essential applications on his desktop.

Timothy spoke about his design strategy in a manner that suggested he was acutely conscious of the implications of these design strategies. For example, describing his desktop environment he commented:

> Okay so this is my default desktop and I'm usually very good about structuring my documents. Everything is perfectly labelled [pointing to the shortcuts to thesis chapters] and for the other folders which I need to make references to, occasionally I put shortcuts to at the very top.... Not visually cluttered by any distractions in the middle ... and in fact the closer they are to the centre the more often I use them. So this imaging tool, which I use most often at the moment [pointing to the tool at the centre] ... it's about where the eye goes to first. If it's in the centre of the screen, that's where it is. These are all time-saving devices. That's the way I work ... I like to have sleekness and elegance.
>
> (Timothy, DPhil psychiatry)

Previously, files, folders and applications could only be accessed by rummaging through the 'start' menu or a hierarchical folder structure – a time-consuming task that interfered with his concentration. The new arrangement not only facilitated ease of access to the tools Timothy used most often, it also provided a symbolic reminder of the importance of each tool for the task at hand. In short, Timothy had designed a desktop environment that delegated the task of managing and regulating his attention to a particular configuration of icons. The whole design process was guided by the principles of 'sleekness' and 'elegance'.

The layout of icons on a virtually desktop only suggests a surface level of design work involved. The task also required Timothy to use a total of sixteen different digital tools to synthesize data sources and produce tables, charts and diagrams that would then be incorporated into the final report written in MS Word. The number of tools involved made considerable demands on the space available on the virtual desktop. Indeed, he lamented the fact that he could not afford a larger monitor to increase the available workspace. However, following a conversation with a friend he had recently downloaded and installed a multiple desktop Powertool; a desktop upgrade that allowed him to switch between four different virtual desktops at the click of a mouse. Consequently, the tool enabled Timothy to switch between workspaces where multiple tools required for particular information processing tasks were immediately available. Having made this design innovation, Timothy estimated he could compile a table from raw brain image data in less than ninety seconds.

This design strategy effectively divided the cognitive labour required to complete each stage of the task into more manageable units. This was evident in the way he described the function and purpose of each desktop environment. He described the first desktop as his 'writing down in a presentable format desktop'. It contained the current dissertation chapter, a virtual 'scratch' pad, a folder full of brain image JPEG files, a chart used for mapping co-ordinates and a PowerPoint slide show (containing selected scans for quick viewing). The second desktop was designated as space for visualization and analysis of raw brain image data. A switch to this space revealed the MRI-Cro application open and running. Desktop three was dedicated to 'looking at those images more closely within the brain' in conjunction with the information contained on a brain imaging website. Finally, desktop four was designated as a space for editing and touching up images (using Corel Draw) that would later be incorporated into dissertation chapters. Overall, the division provided a 'visual way of categorizing tasks' and allowed him to offload the cognitive load required to complete each task to the predesigned desktop environment.

Tim was extremely proud of this recent design innovation. He argued that it had resulted in considerable productivity gains and accelerated his capacity to task-switch. To invoke a theatrical metaphor, a tap of the shortcut key set the stage for a particular act.[3] With the stage set with all the props and scaffolds ready to hand, Tim was able step into role and enact a specific part in an ongoing performance. In effect the multi-desktop Powertool broke down the task in more manageable units. Each desktop enable Tim to offload the cognitive load for completing specific tasks to a predesigned environment. In this manner he was able to accelerate and expand his capacity to engage in the complex and challenging task of brain image analysis

Interestingly, Timothy invested a lot of time fine-tuning his desktop environment. Nevertheless, rapid completion of the thesis, rather than deep understanding, appeared to motivate this design strategy. Indeed, he admitted that he had managed to automate the process to the extent that he did not always understand the meanings of the interpretations, graphs and tables produced. In fact, follow-up interviews revealed that he had grown weary of clinical research and had applied to retrain as a medical doctor. Moreover, he had to submit his thesis by the end of the summer as a precondition of his acceptance to medical school. This deadline was absolute and the pressure created seemed to permeate every aspect of his practice.

The vignette illustrates an important general principle. Before a learner can engage in advanced knowledge work using digital tools and resources they must design a cognitive ecology to support advanced knowledge work. The same principle applies to study-related practices involving traditional tools and resources. Nevertheless, there are only so many ways non-virtual resources can be arranged and configured on a physical desktop. In contrast, the digital domain affords new design opportunities and new design challenges. Indeed learners can no longer depend on the intelligence designed into a physical desktop environment. Advanced knowledge work invariably involves the use of dozens of digital tools in multiple combinations and demands that students take on more of the responsibility for customizing their environment for the task at hand. In short, in the new media age the learner is *compelled* to engage in the work of design. The vignette also suggests that effective design must be understood not only in terms of the achievement of a particular outcome (i.e. completing a dissertation) but also with respect to the conditions under which this outcome must be achieved (e.g. Timothy's need to submit by a certain date). In this respect, microlevel design decisions are inextricably related to wider contextual factors; in this case the career trajectory that Timothy envisaged for himself. Both required a considerable degree of foresight and conscious reflection.

The scope of design work in the new media age

Design work involves far more than selecting different styles of visual layout and has implications for every aspect of practice. Expert-like designers anticipate the implications and design with the aim of increasing productivity in various ways. For example, ZeroGBoy had deliberately removed icons from the tool bar menu on Microsoft Word to force himself to use shortcut keys – a strategy which he estimated would result in more a more efficient working practice. Similarly, Ardash transferred subscription to multiple e-mail listservs to an RSS feed reader to reduce the clutter in his e-mail inbox. In general, the analysis of students' desktops revealed that dozens of design decisions had been made; decisions about: default templates; auto-save timings; backup schedules; e-mail arrival notifications; RSS feed subscriptions; and decisions about file arrangements. Furthermore, it is important to understand design work as an ongoing activity rather than a phase that precedes the execution of a particular task.

A second vignette serves to illustrate how a capacity for interactive design within a digital domain enhances a student's capacity to engage in the production of legalistic discourse. Here, the work of design is shown to be an ongoing and dynamic process. Moreover, it starts to suggest how design work impacted upon a student's capacity to visualize data, see patterns, and assemble information. Further, the vignette suggests why these digitally mediated practices had implications for Jim's capacity to make original and scholarly contributions to a competitive academic field.

Vignette: Jim mashing-up a legal essay

Jim had designed a sophisticated virtual filing cabinet that helped him manage and access a complex system of notes that he could draw upon rapidly to produce highly stylized legal documents that demonstrated his extensive subject knowledge. He chose to organize his notes thematically, grouping notes into themes such as 'democratizing resource scarcity' and 'polycentricity'. He also created folders of notes organized in terms of 'cases', 'articles' and 'legislation'. This was an important part of his information storage and visualization strategy. As he searched, browsed and read articles and case histories on the West Law database, the representational structure allowed him to access relevant notes files within seconds and write (or cut and paste) information into the relevant file. In this respect, the process of making and filing the notes (which remain distinct activities in the paper-based world) had been conflated into an integrated activity. Further, the activity of organizing and 'theming' notes became integral to the more creative work of planning and writing. In short, note taking, for Jim had become a creative and expressive process, akin to an art form, that allowed him to make connections, identify issues and see alternative ways of conceptualizing legalistic problems. Jim went on to publish several papers in high impact law journals in his second year as a postgraduate student.

The process of making and filing notes may not be peculiar to the digital domain. However, Jim's practice suggests that the ease with which note files could be accessed, selected, cut and pasted and rearranged introduced a dynamism and fluidity into the process that is absent in the paper-based world. Indeed, it appears that in the age of digital media, the practice of academic law involves design work invisible to the reader of legal essays. Moreover, these microlevel design strategies can empower individuals to engage with and perform in competitive academic fields.

The challenges and choices confronting the learner as designer

Both vignettes introduced suggest some of the cognitive advances afforded by effective design work. However, it is also important to emphasize that design work is an expansive activity, fraught with tensions and contradictions, that requires students to continually monitor, speculate and calculate the benefits and drawbacks of specific design innovations. Two key challenges confronting the learner as designer concern the challenge of designing alone without guidance and the problem of conflicting design objectives.

Designing alone

A capacity for effective design is a prerequisite for advanced study in the new media age. Nevertheless, learners are invariably engaged in the work of design without any kind of guidance. Timothy was extremely frustrated that he had had to devise a system for analysing brain image data almost entirely on his own. He commented:

> I've had no help with this and no single person has told me how to find out where brain activations are or how to find out what to do – no one has told me any of this! That might be the idea of a [doctorate], but that just hacks me off. There's someone next door probably, they know exactly what to do but they don't want to spend the time. What I dislike most is all of the tools that I use are so spread out. As far as I'm concerned there should be one program into which you put in your raw data and it gives you a table just like that. It should also refer to a database on what those brain regions do. That would be ideal for me and that's the kind of thing I would love to make myself because it's all about the synthesis of it all, that's my thing. But if I don't know a program exists. I can't find it and what annoys me about this is that everyone is reinventing the wheel.
>
> (Timothy, DPhil psychiatry)

In lieu of an integrated analysis system, he was forced to invest considerable time and energy designing and customizing the virtual environment for the task at hand, a process he described as 'reinventing the wheel'. In short, he was compelled to design and to design alone.

One might suppose that students who live in college cultures enjoy more opportunities than most to share innovative practice and learning from peers. However, the study suggested that individual students might remain wholly unaware of the design innovations made by others, even those working on similar tasks. This problem might be compounded by a trend for students to spend more time working alone in their study rooms in relative isolation.

Nevertheless, some students who routinely worked in the same computer room or particular library remained wholly unaware of strategies used by their peers. Again, this highlights the degree to which students are compelled to design alone. Indeed, until tools are invented that make the process of design more visible, it seems likely that design work of this kind will remain a rather private, if not secretive affair.

Conflicting design objectives

Students' desktop environments are designed to support a range of social, recreational and everyday life management tasks as well as study-related activities. As a result, the challenge of designing a cognitive ecology to support advanced knowledge work is often compounded by the existence of conflicting design objectives. For example, Edina and Miss Lullaby admitted 'wasting' hours chatting to friends on MSN Instant Messenger. Jacqueline, who described herself as an 'eBay junkie', frequently treated herself to some virtual 'retail therapy' by entering online auctions for fun. Others reported 'wasting time' looking for cheap flights and checking out other people's music collections on iTunes. All students complained that the constant flow of administrative e-mail into their inboxes had interfered with their capacity to study.

In practice, the challenge of maintaining a boundary between study space and recreational space manifested itself in a variety of ways. For example, Ardash discussed organizing his daily routine into distinct sections and allocating time when he was not allowed to check e-mail or read news. Likewise, Edina chose to use a paper-based diary and wall planner for personal organization and planning rather than Microsoft Outlook which was installed on her computer. Similarly, Katrina started to go to the library and deliberately leave her Ethernet cable at home to resist the temptation to surf the net whilst studying. In these cases, students appeared to self-impose enabling constraints that helped them avoid potential web-based distractions.

In Sue Ellen's case, the separation of roles was taken to an extreme. She owned an iMac that she used extensively to 'chat' to friends, share-music, participate in the Friendster community and shop when in her study room. However, she chose to conduct most of her course work on a computer in the college computer room (situated beneath her bedroom). She remarked: 'The computer downstairs is kind of neutral; it's free of distractions'. This strategy enabled her to focus on a single study related task like writing an essay free of the constant temptation to shop or socialize. Again, she demonstrated a capacity to regulate her own attention, from the outside, by strategically separating her computer use for work and play. However, for most students the collapse in the separation of distinct boundaries between study space and leisure space posed considerable challenges.

Towards a theory of mindful design

It is important to understand the processes that shape the design of learners' personalized learning environments over time. To this end, I offer a three-tier typology that encourages us to understand the work of design in terms of different agencies that contribute to the design of a personal learning environment. I refer to these design states as inherited designs, evolved designs and mindful designs. I believe this typology can help us better understand how students' personalized learning environments evolve over time.

Inherited designs

Inherited designs are dominated by default settings inherited from the installation of the operating system and exhibit minimal evidence of conscious design work. In this respect, the bulk of the design work has been inherited from decisions made by designers and usability engineers who work for software manufacturers. All desktop environments exhibit the personal imprint of the user to greater or lesser degrees. However, in selected desktop environments evidence of inherited design work is more conspicuous. For example, Ishani's desktop resembled the desktop of a machine with a default installation. There was little surface evidence of customization and her browser's 'favourite' folder only contained six links. Further, it appeared as if applications had automatically installed many of the icons visible on her computers virtual desktop. This is not to say that Ishani had not started to design her desktop environment. There was simply limited evidence to suggest that she had designed and customized her virtual environment to support specific kinds of knowledge work. In this respect, the notion of inherited design directs our attention to the intelligence inherited from the designers of digital tools as opposed to the intelligence designed into a personal learning environment by the users themselves.

Evolved designs

In practice all desktop designs evolve over time, beginning from the installation of an operating system as students start to use their computers for specific purposes. Evolved designs manifest themselves in students' choice of wallpaper, the layout of icons, links accessible in 'favourite' menus and instant messenger 'buddy lists'. In effect, the category 'evolved design' serves to describe personalized learning environments that manifest evidence of their user's attempts to adapt, modify and customize default settings. However, this category is reserved for just-in-time and on-demand design work that users perform in order to address specific needs as they arise. In this respect, evolved designs must be understood as the product of a continuous process of design and adaptation rather than conscious reflection. A capacity to adapt and engage in the work of design 'on the fly' in this manner might be considered a basic form of new media literacy. Nevertheless, what remains interesting (as illustrated in both vignettes described above) is what an advanced practitioner does over and above this process of just-in-time adaptation.

Mindful designs

I conceptualize desktop environments that manifest a high degree of conscious design work as mindful designs. Students who monitor their own study-related practices recognize the tensions and contradictions inherent in those practices, and actively redesign their cognitive ecologies in an attempt to overcome these tensions, are conceived as mindful designers. Mindfully designed desktop environments are not, on the surface, distinguishable from evolved designs. The distinction concerns the degree of conscious reflection involved in the design process.

Both Timothy and Jim were mindful designers. Each took time to reflect on their tool-mediated practice and identified tensions and contradictions inhibiting their capacity to engage in specific object-orientated activities. Furthermore, each executed design innovations in order to enhance productivity, amplifying their capacity to engage in advanced knowledge work. Significantly, both Timothy and Jim had clearly defined design objectives and worked to tight deadlines. Timothy's design work was guided by the principles of 'sleekness' and 'elegance'. Jim's design work was finely honed to support the production of a specific form of legalistic discourse. In each case, evidence of mindful design was manifest in the self-conscious articulation of their specific design rationales rather than the particular configuration of tools observed.

A capacity for mindful design depends upon students' knowledge of the tools and resources available, and the tools and resources required for the task at hand. Interestingly, Kress (2003) argues that 'the sculptor must know the potentials of this kind of wood, of that kind of stone, of these metals, of silicone and of fibreglass' (p. 24). He adds, the 'designer must know what resources will best meet the demands of a specific design for a specific audience' (ibid.). The argument applies equally to the designer of a cognitive ecology. Knowledge of the available tools, and their particular constraints and affordances, are necessary before one can engage in the work of design. Nevertheless, a user must also learn how to configure the available resources for their immediate and specific purposes. In this respect, mindful design involves a capacity to customize or reconfigure a cognitive ecology for the particular task at hand. Interestingly, Kress also argues:

> in a world of instability, reproduction is no longer an issue: what is required now is the ability to assess what is needed in this situation now, for these conditions, these purposes, this audience – all of which will be differently configured for the next task
>
> (op. cit.: 49)

These words might also capture something essential about challenges confronting students designing personalized learning environments.

To become a mindful designer, a learner needs to become more self-conscious about the various ways cognitive processes are mediated by a designed environment. I call this more general capacity mindfulness, simply defined as a capacity to become aware of the mediated nature of one's practice in any given cognitive ecology. Unlike the more familiar term of meta-cognition (Biggs 1988; Metcalfe and Shimamura 1994) or reflective practice (Schön 1983, 1987), the concept of mindfulness is premised on an understanding that cognition is distributed among the quasi-virtual ecologies that learners design to engage in advanced knowledge work.

In summary, a capacity for mindful design enables learners to customize their working environments for a particular task, monitor their own practice and strategically redesign the environment, if and when required, to support advanced knowledge work. Optimal designs for any particular task only exist as an elusive ideal state. Nevertheless, mindful designers appear to possess a capacity to adapt, modify and customize designs over time with a clear sense of purpose.

Emotive designs, mindfulness and designs for social futures

Design work manifest in desktop environments is not always motivated by a need to engage in advanced knowledge work. Social, recreational and life management needs also generate design objectives that, in turn, impact upon design strategies employed. Furthermore, non-study-related activities cannot always be bracketed off as a potential source of distraction. Design decisions made for social and motivational reasons may have important implications for a student's capacity to engage in concentrated study. For example, Edina set a photograph of herself surrounded by friends celebrating the completion of her exams as the background wallpaper on her laptop. The bright and colourful imagery, including balloons and popping champagne bottles, obscured some of the shortcuts to functional applications on her desktop. However, she liked the photo and said it made her 'feel good'. In short, the emotional support provided by the image took priority over the need to design a visually elegant and efficient desktop environment for study. Similarly, Jacqueline described how, when feeling homesick, she set up a direct Skype connection to a computer in her parental home in Paris so she could talk to her 'mum' and then left it on, all day long, so she could overhear conversations in her family kitchen. In this case she had appropriated an affordance of a newly accessible technology – free Internet telephony – to import a sense of home and family into her Oxford study room to ward off homesickness.

In certain cases, tools for study- and non-study-related tasks were consciously combined. For example, Timothy placed the shortcut to Google Earth in the centre of his desktop workspace to provide quick access to a virtual space that he used for a virtual study break rather than take a physical (and potentially time-consuming) break away from his computer. The tool allowed him to fly around the globe and zoom in on one of his twenty or more favourite places. Demonstrating the use of the tool, he commented:

> I'm just taking myself off to my favourite places in the world. I don't know if you've been to Venice, I have, it's a wonderful place and I just need to get away for a bit so I'll double click on Venice ... this is where I go when I can't get out of my office!
>
> (Timothy, DPhil psychiatry)

He also had saved shortcuts to the Grand Canyon, Niagara Falls, New York, Toronto, Inside Mount St Helens and Bill Gates' house. Thus, Google Earth had become a tool that Timothy used to help relax in between periods of intense concentration.

These observations suggest the limitations of conceiving of the learner's desktop environment as a cognitive ecology to support advanced knowledge work. Indeed, they lead us to a more holistic understanding of a virtually figured world that has implications for their emotional states, which are in turn bound up with their sense of self and community. In this respect, the concept of mindfulness is premised on an understanding that virtual ecologies mediate a learner's emotional and affective states, as well as their capacity to engage in advanced knowledge work. Furthermore, these emotional and effective states appear inextricably related to the ways students design virtual environments that place them in a particular relation to other people who in turn shape their sense of self and community. These insights are developed in Chapters 5 and 6.

Summary

This chapter draws attention to the practice of designing a cognitive ecology to support advanced knowledge work as a fundamental aspect of new media literacy. In a paper-based environment, one's capacity to play an active role in customizing and designing one's desktop environment is relatively restricted. In contrast, in the new media age students are compelled to engage in the work of design. This chapter illustrates *mindful designers* cultivating cognitive ecologies to amplify their capacity to engage in advanced knowledge work. However, it also draws attention to the challenge of designing alone, managing conflicting design objectives and negotiating the collapse in the traditional boundaries between study space and recreational space. Finally, this chapter suggests the need to consider how designed virtual environments mediate learners' emotive and affective states.

4 Creative appropriation, new media and self-education

If we could rid ourselves of all pride, if, to define our species, we kept strictly to what the historic and prehistoric periods show us to be the constant characteristic of man and of intelligence, we should say not *Homo sapiens* but *Homo faber*. In short, intelligence, considered in what seems to be its original feature, is the faculty of manufacturing artificial objects, especially tools for making tools, and of indefinitely varying the manufacture.

(Henry Bergson 1983 [1911]: 139, cited in Wertsch *et al.* 1995: 20)

Sly as a fox and twice as quick, there are countless ways of 'making do'.

(de Certeau 1988, p. 29)

Introduction

Learners are agentic. They seek out new mediational means to advance their purposes. From a sociocultural perspective, this is part of what makes us human. Cole and Derry (2005) emphasize this point in an essay entitled *We are Technology and It is Us*. The paper starts with a meditation on the symbolism of the memorable 'Dawn of Man' sequence from *2001: A Space Odyssey* (Kubrick 1968). The sequence depicts a pre-historic apeman discovering that the bone of a dead animal can be used as a weapon. The symbolism of the scene implies that *Homo sapiens*, or *Homo faber* as Bergson recommends, started to pull away from other species in the evolutionary struggle for survival through the creative use of tools that extended their physical capabilities.

In the information age, postgraduate students have little need for tools that might be used as weapons, nor for tools that extend their physical capabilities. However, advanced knowledge work is making ever-increasing demands on the biological brain and students find themselves under increasing pressure to seek out new tools and explore how they might be used to extend cognitive functioning. If they cannot find them, they seek to make new ones. As Bergson notes, 'tools that make tools' are especially useful in this respect. In the interim, students are adept at 'making do' with the tools at their disposal.

In educational contexts, we know that an increasing number of young people look to the Web, rather than to the library, as a resource bank of study aids. Lenhart *et al.* note this trend, quoting a child who, to the dismay of librarians, argued:

> Without the Internet you need to go to the library and walk around looking for books. In today's world you can just go home and get into the Internet and type in your search term. The results are endless. There is so much information that you have to ignore a lot of it.
>
> (Lenhart *et al.* 2001: 4)

Websites and online services that cater explicitly for the study needs of school and university students included: portal sites (including links to other educational resources); articles and information sites relating to specific topics; sites for buying selling and sharing essays; 'Ask an Expert' sites; sites containing book notes and summaries; online encyclopaedias; and sites offering online tutoring services (op. cit.: 5–7). Similarly (Jones 2002: 13) found that 'an overwhelming number of students reported that the Internet, rather than the library, is the primary site of their information searches'. Three-quarters (73 per cent) of college students said they use the Internet more than the library and four-fifths (80 per cent) of college students reported using the library less than three hours per week. These mixed method studies identify interesting trends. However, figures like these might no longer surprise.

This chapter aims to understand why students might turn to the Web for resources and the degree to which web-based instructional resources complement, replace or undermine students' dependence on traditional learning media. It draws upon data collected through stimulated responses collected as students actually used digital tools in real time (see Appendix). Data produced through surveys, focus groups, and student self-report can only provide limited insights in this respect.

The concept of creative appropriation expanded

The notion of appropriation emphasizes an irreducible tension between the intentions of the tool user and the resistance offered by the tool. This way of thinking derives from the work of Bakhtin and colleagues who stresses that speakers are constantly struggling to express themselves by appropriating the words of others:

> The word in language is half someone else's. It becomes 'one's own' only when the speaker populates it with his own intention, his own accent, when he appropriates the word, adapting it to his own semantic and expressive intention. Prior to this moment of appropriation, the word does not exist in a neutral and impersonal language (it is not, after all, out of a dictionary that the speaker gets his words) but rather it exists in other

people's mouths, in other people's contexts, serving other people's intentions: it is from there that one must take a word, and make it one's own.

(Bakhtin 1981: 293–294)

This provides a useful model for thinking about the various ways learners
populate digital tools with their own intentions, adapt them to serve their
own purposes, and misuse tools in ways not intended by the designers to
serve their own purposes. Indeed, the concept of *creative appropriation* foregrounds the agency of learners as they start to reach out and find digital tools
and resources to mediate their own goal-directed learning activities. In addition, it encourages us to see the Internet, not unlike Bakhtin conceived of
spoken language, as a site of struggle in which contradictory agendas are at
work shaping the agency of the learner.

The concept of creative appropriation highlights the creativity, ingenuity
and resourcefulness of advanced learners as they discover, experiment with
and explore the affordances of web-based tools. De Certeau's work on *The
Practice of Everyday Life* provides a source of inspiration and a useful distinction between producer 'strategies' and consumer 'tactics' that have proved
useful in this respect. Indeed, his work continually stresses the resourcefulness of consumers as they employ tactics to subvert the strategies of produc-
ers to achieve their purposes. For example, he writes:

> In reality, a rationalized, expansionist, centralized, spectacular and clam-
> orous production is confronted by an entirely different kind of produc-
> tion, called 'consumption' and characterized by its ruses, its
> fragmentation (the results of circumstance), its poaching, its clandestine
> nature, its tireless but quiet activity, in short by its quasi-invisibility,
> since it shows itself not in its own products (where would it place
> them?) but in an art of using these imposed upon it.
>
> (de Certeau 1988: 31)

In this respect, the notion of creative appropriation, conceived as a heuristic,
focuses attention on some of the invisible and clandestine ways learners are
subverting the intentions of commercial enterprises, tactically poaching
web-based resources resources and using tools *against the grain* in ways not
intended by designers to expand learning opportunities. This capacity might
be regarded as a core new media literacy required to exploit the full potential of the Internet as a resource for learning given the dizzying array of
freely available online tools and services produced by commercial organizations and not-for-profit organizations.

Breaking away from the traditional university

In this chapter the concept of *creative appropriation* is also associated with
Engeström's (1987, 1996) notion of 'breaking away'. In Chapter 2 I discussed

how expansive learning theory can sensitize us to instances in which individuals start to radically question the context of action, recognize that they are in a *double bind* and start to transform the context of action. The vignettes presented below draw attention to the diverse ways students are now breaking away from a dependence on traditional tools and resources administered by centralized computer services and turning to the Internet as the primary site of (self) instruction. The strategies employed by Anastasia to teach herself multivariate analysis provides a good example. It shows how Anastasia creatively appropriates a variety of web-based resources to break away from a prior dependence on formal instruction and creates an alternative context that allows her to advance an independent (self) directed learning agenda. In this respect, this section starts to illustrate why we might be witnessing the decentring of the traditional university and opens up a window into the future of (self) education.

Vignette: Anastasia teachers herself statistics

Anastasia was following a taught MSc course in evidence-based social work. Modules on statistical analysis were compulsory. However, she had no background in either statistics or mathematics and found the course extremely challenging. The statistics course was conducted in a seminar room by a lecturer who made extensive use of paper-based handouts. Asked about her experience of the course, Anastasia complained:

> It wasn't very helpful for me, not only for me but for several of us on the course. We had never done statistics and found it difficult ... because this system with handouts, learning statistics on handouts, it wasn't very good for me – the Professor would come with handouts that would have ANOVA and under ANOVA he'd have the SPSS table but I did not see how he did it or what all these figures meant. And he'd say 'you can see from this ANOVA test that this number is significant'. I would think, why is this significant? What does this mean? This is all completely useless to me!
>
> (Anastasia, MSc Social Policy)

The course did include sessions in a computer room in which students used the SPSS statistical analysis software package to analyse pre-compiled datasets. However, Anastasia argued that the lectures had jumped ahead so fast she had not acquired the basic conceptual building blocks she needed to progress. This was a tremendous source of frustration. She had taken the course in evidence-based social work because she firmly believed that a more scientific body of evidence was required to inform policy and practice. So much so, that, despite the difficulties she was experiencing, she was one of only two students on her course to opt for a dissertation project that involved the use of multi-linear regression modelling. Consequently, she found herself caught in a double bind: it was essential that she learn and understand how to use the ANOVA test, but the lectures and seminars on her course left her feeling utterly confused.

Having abandoned hope that she could learn statistics via formal instruction, Anastasia took matters into her own hands. She started to teach herself statistics with the aid of web-based instructional materials. Rather than relying on a few general websites (recommended in her book), Anastasia found relevant resources by 'Googling' the name of particular tests. A simple Google search for ANOVA returned dozens of links to resources dealing explicitly with the analysis of variance tests. She remarked that 'one in five' links returned information directly related to her current needs, but added that many of the sites were too complicated for her to grasp at first. She did, however, select websites judged suitable for her evolving needs and created a shortcut via a folder in her browser's favourites menu. In this way, Anastasia gradually built up a folder of valued online resources. Some sites provided interactive demonstrations of core concepts, others provided worked examples and others provided more abstract expositions on the theme of multiple linear regression. She developed a clear idea of the relative utility of each resource in her favourites folder.

When using these resources she switched back and forth between resources exploiting the affordances specific to each: a clear explanation, a particular helpful diagram or a helpful screen shot sequence demonstrating how to conduct specific ANOVA tests using SPSS. In one procedure, she switched between three or four online resources and a book, *SPSS for Social Scientists*,

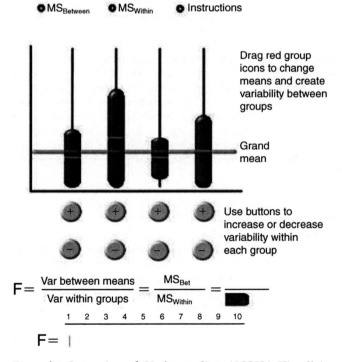

Figure 4.1 Screenshot of 'Understanding ANOVA Visually' website (source: Thomas Malloy, University of Utah).

whilst simultaneously attempting to apply the test on her own data set on the SPSS program installed on her computer. Indeed, web-based instruction informed practices but problems encountered whilst attempting to apply the test also inspired her to seek further explanation from both online and offline resources.

Interestingly, in the early stages she found the *Understanding ANOVA Visually* website particularly useful. The diagrammatic representation helped Anastasia acquire a holistic conceptualization of the ANOVA concept. Initially she attempted to understand the test by applying it to her own data set using SPSS. In short, through a process of search and experimentation, she found a web-based resource that equipped her with a cognitive tool that enabled her to develop a mature conceptualizing of the ANOVA test.[1] In turn, this enabled her to complete her project, complete a dissertation using advanced statistical analysis techniques and go on to become a fully qualified evidence-based social worker capable of conducting statistical analysis involving regression modelling.

This vignette illustrates how a student appropriated web-based tools to escape a double bind and break away from traditional modes of learning and instruction. In the seminar room, Anastasia could not proceed given the particular configuration of tools and resources at her disposal. Instructional materials were provided, but the locus of control for managing the learning experience remained with the lecturer. As a result, the pace of the lesson and level of scaffolding provided were imposed from the outside. In contrast, when teaching herself statistics on the web, the locus of control remained with the learner. Within the personalized learning environment she has created on her own computer Anastasia could choose between multiple web-based instructional materials pitched at different levels, and use different representational formats, if and when required, to address her changing learning needs. In short, access to freely available web-based instructional materials empowered Anastasia to position herself within a zone of proximal development. In turn, the personalized learning environment that she had designed empowered Anastasia to advance a self-directed learning agenda relatively independently of the traditional university. In this respect, access to new media empowered her to escape a double bind and break away into a quasi-virtual context of her own figuration.

Anastasia's story was not typical. Few students found themselves in such a predicament. However, many had started to appropriate new media to complement and expand existing learning strategies. The next vignettes shows how a student starts to exploit some free web-based tools to expand his existing repertoire of literature searching strategies. In this example, we witness a student playfully exploring how a newly discovered web-based resources that had not been intentionally designed to support learning, might be used *against the grain* as a learning resource.

Vignette: Ardash appropriates Amazon.com for literature searching

Amazon.com allows the user to read independent third party book reviews uploaded by other users and see all other works published by the same author. Further, the book recommendation system exploits a crowd sourcing technique to make personalized recommendations based on an analysis of the purchasing decisions of others who bought the book the user is currently looking at. In effect, the collective intelligence of thousands of anonymous others harvested by the book recommendation system guides and directs the attention of the user.

Ardash had started to use Amazon.com in combination with Oxford Library Information System (OLIS) for conducting literature searches. He found the book recommendation system particularly useful. It allowed him rapidly discover all books published by the same author, follow links to books published by co-authors and serendipitously discover books that, he argued, you would not find on the same shelf in a bookshop. Indeed, he argued that the book recommendation system had helped him develop a more holistic insight into the 'multiple webs of influence' between authors. Nevertheless, Ardash was cautious not to allow the book recommendation system to manipulate him. Discussing his use of the resource he remarked: 'I look at the recommendations but I feel like there is an agenda that is not mine so I don't often buy upon recommendation.' Interestingly however he did not use it primarily to buy books. He stressed:

> I'll search a book in Amazon and then find out what it is about and whether it's worth reading ... it's much easier on Amazon than on the web or on OLIS or anything else. So in many ways it is the first step in acquiring a book, whether it is in the library or online. It is one additional step before wasting your time and going to the library and actually reading it.
>
> (Ardash, DPhil Medical Anthropology)

In short, he was exploiting an affordance of the tool but resisting the commercial agenda that that the tool was designed to serve.

Following his initial use Ardash soon started to discover additional ways to use Amazon.com to support learning. One tactic exploited the affordances of the 'Search Inside Me' tool; a tool that allows readers to open a virtual representation of a book, read back pages, contents pages and search for specific words or phrases. He had discovered a use for the tool in India conducting field research and promptly e-mailed to announce the discovery:

> Hey
> I'm writing to let you in on a trick I figured out. Because it's quite difficult to get recent academic books in India, I had to find alternative means. Amazon has just begun a new feature of searching keywords inside books. Especially for better selling books, they offer this service. It basically allows you to find all the instances of a word you chose and lets

you see that page and two pages subsequent. If you, therefore, pick the keyword 'Introduction' you can read the first three pages. Then, you pick a word on that third page and you can read the next two pages and so on. By using this trick (that I don't think they thought about), I've almost completed two chapters of a recently published book! If not for reading the whole thing, it's a great way to get a feel for some major authors and books before you go buy them.

To have access to this service, I believe you need to have bought something from Amazon previously or just sign-up. And then, find the book you're interested in and under the title, if the service is available, it will say 'search inside.' Try it out!

(Ardash, DPhil Medical Anthropology)

Later Ardash discovered that he could use the 'Search Inside Me' tool to search for specific words or phrases. Upon his return from India, this proved especially useful for finding the page number of missing references. Indeed he discovered that it was frequently faster to use the tool to find a particular quotation that he needed even if he had a paper-based version of the book ready to hand. Thus, in this context, Amazon.com became a powerful tool that supported the activity of scholarly writing.

The case of Ardash illustrates a student exploring and playfully tinkering with a tool to explore how it might be tactically redeployed to serve his changing needs. It encourages us to consider how the use of a new tool pushes back and starts to shape the practices, objectives and motives of the tool users. For example, when Ardash's used Amazon.com to extend his existing repertoire of literature searching strategies, the tool pushed back and stimulated an interest in the 'webs of influence' between authors. In this case, the appropriation and use of new tools did not simply extend an individual's capacity to achieve their purposes, it actually shaped and reorganized these pre-existing interests and stimulated new interests. In this respect, creative appropriation might be understood as a transformative process that is reconfiguring the culture practices of private study.

The case of Anastasia and that of Ardash also illustrate students exploiting access to web-based tools to develop radically personalized self-directed learning agendas relatively independently of the traditional university. Anastasia turned to the Internet out of necessity to escape a double bind. In contrast, Ardash turned to the Internet to expand learning opportunities and seek efficiency gains. Either way, both had authentic needs that were not being addressed by tools and services accessible through the traditional university. Both found freely available digital tools and resources accessible through the Internet could be used to address these needs. Both set about creating a cognitive ecology that gave them more control over the learning process and both became less dependent on the traditional university as a result. In this respect, accessing new media facilitated a *shift in the locus of agency for regulating and managing learning.*

Creative appropriation and authentic need

In order to understand what motivates learners to appropriate new tools as learning resources it is also important to identify the authentic learning need that any single act of creative appropriation helps to satisfy. Indeed, where existing resources address students' learning needs, creative appropriations are unlikely to occur. For example, Ishani's needs as a medical student were adequately catered for by the tools and resource made available through Web Learn, the institutional Virtual Learning Environment (VLE). However, when these needs are not meet, as this chapter reveals, resourceful learners are appropriating digital tools in surprising and unexpected ways. Nevertheless, in order to understand any particular act of creative appropriation it is important to understand the particular configuration of sociocultural and historical circumstances that gives rise to the need. ZeroGBoy's use of G-mail as a backup tool serves to clarify this point.

Vignette: ZeroGBoys use of Gmail as backup service

ZeroGBoy, a student of environmental education, was edging closer towards the completion of his doctoral studies. He was in the process of writing up, drafting and continually redrafting chapters. The threat of data loss due to hard drive failure, accidental deletion or theft had become a source of considerably anxiety. As a result, he had developed multiple strategies to guard against data loss. Initially he had considered purchasing an external hard drive. However, he figured that this could be stolen along with his computer. He then started to made regular backups on a USB memory stick that he kept on his person at all times. Nevertheless, he remained concerned that his memory stick might be lost and decided that it was important to make additional backups online. At first he explored possibility of using the TSM backup service provided by the university computer services. However, the service involved the use of password protected security procedures and could take hours to run. His access to the service also depended on his affiliation to the university, which he would no longer have after graduation. Consequently, he developed a somewhat unusual, but extremely effective alternative back-up strategy that exploited the affordances of a free online resource.

Following an invitation from a friend, ZeroGBoy had opened a free Gmail (Google Mail) account. He had no need for an additional e-mail account. However, it allowed him to store over a gigabyte of digitized files as attachments. He identified this as a free resource that he could exploit to address an authentic need. He then started e-mailing himself a copy of the chapter he was working on at the end of each day. This ensured he had dated copies of all versions of each chapter in an online storage location that could be retrieved from any computer in the world in the event of hard drive failure, computer theft or the loss of the USB memory stick. It also provided a free alternative to centralized TMS back-up service administered by centralized computer services that would require him to go through irritating security procedures and that he would not be able to access if he ceased to be a member of the university.

The vignette suggests one way in which a student might exploit a new tool against the grain in a manner not intended by the designers to address an authentic need. In this case, four factors appeared to be involved in ZeroG-Boy's decision to appropriate Gmail as a free offline storage location for backing up thesis chapters: (a) the accessibility of the tool; (b) the fact that it offered a free alternative to buying an external hard drive; (c) the additional security of knowing he had a copy of his chapters in an offline location that could be neither lost, nor stolen; and (d) that fact that these were automatically dated and could be easily retrieved, if need be, from any computer. Thus, this case illustrates how a specific act of creative appropriation is motivated by a range of interconnected needs; needs that are related to a particular configuration of sociocultural and historical circumstances.

Appropriations and tactical redeployments

Students appropriate tools to address very specific learning needs at particular points in time. However, tools discovered for one purpose might be tactically redeployed over time for quite different purposes. Karen's use of web-based chemistry resources for her work as a trainee teacher provides an interesting case in point. It suggests that creative appropriation involves a capacity to seek out opportunities for tactical redeployments as they arise.

Vignette: Karen's use of ChemFinder

Karen did the bulk of her resourcing on the Web. She often scanned through multiple chemistry websites and 'cherry picked' tools and resources that she later incorporated into her own lessons/presentations. These were also shared in an online depository with other chemistry teachers on her course. In this manner she radically assembled a re-usable bank of digital tools and resources. Karen found a tool called ChemFinder particularly useful. The tool allowed her find all the information she required about specific chemicals (i.e. molecular weight, boiling point, water solubility) with a few clicks of the mouse. Further, links to diagrammatic representations of chemical structures provided further opportunities to develop her subject knowledge.

Karen had started to use ChemFinder whilst studying chemistry as an undergraduate. However, as a trainee teacher, she now routinely used it to prepare lessons or to check the results of students' work. She argued that the tool saved her hours. Later she discovered that some of the students in her classes had discovered and started to use the tool to assist with their homework. At first she was concerned that the students might use the tool to cheat when doing their homework. However, she figured that there was little, if anything, she could do about it, and subsequently started to devise e-tivities (Salmon 2002) that required students to make use ChemFinder in combination with an interactive version of the periodic table of the elements. In time Karen started to form judgments about the relative utility of each tool for different groups and ability ranges. For example, she argued that ChemFinder was really a professional tool suitable for A-level students, whereas the interactive periodic table of the elements could be easily used by students of the ages.

The vignette shows how a trainee teacher tactically redeployed a tool she had started to use as an undergraduate to address her changing needs as she embarked upon her career. Further, it suggests the need to think about creative appropriation as a capacity to actively seek out opportunities to deploy and redeploy tools over time for different purposes to maximize their utility in different circumstances. Indeed a capacity to mindfully monitor their own use of tools and constantly seek out new opportunities for tactical redeployments appears to be a distinctive quality of expert-like practice and a important aspect of new media literacy. In short, new media literacy requires a capacity for continual adaptation and preparedness to make tactical redeployments. The vignette also suggests that students who always depend on tools, resources and practices with which they become familiar as students could find themselves at a distinct disadvantage as they progress into the world of work.

Creative appropriation: driving cultural change from the bottom up

All the examples introduced so far illustrate students breaking away from a dependence on traditional tools and resources. Significantly, in each case, students appropriated digital tools because they allowed them to address authentic needs and expand learning opportunities. Importantly, access to new technologies does not cause change in itself. These students innovate new practices that exploit the affordances of digital technologies to address authentic learning needs and enhance their capacity to study. I believe this process has already started to drive systemic change in the culture of higher education; a process that is now resulting in the decentring of the traditional university. In order to clarify this point it is helpful to zoom out and consider how creative appropriations on a microgenetic level might be driving cultural change from the bottom up. This requires a short digression.

Scholars interested in the relationship between cultural and media change invariably become embroiled in a debate that polarizes two camps: those accused of technological determinists, often linked with the work of Marshal McLuhan (1962; McLuhan and Lapham 1994); and advocates of the *Social Shaping of Technology* who emphasize that technologies are always invented and adapted by real people in particular socio-historical circumstances (MacKenzie and Wajcman 1999). Sociocultural theory provides a third way to think about the implications of media change that stems from the centrality of the idea of the dialectic in work influenced by Vygotsky and the Soviet school.

Wertsch (1998: 23–72; 1995: 65–68) develops this line of thinking using an analogy that makes reference to the history of pole-vaulting following the invention of fibreglass. He describes how a small group of young athletes develop new techniques that exploited the elasticity of fibreglass poles in order to gain a competitive advantage. With the aid of the new fibreglass poles the young vaulters could slingshot themselves over the bar and far surpass the records set by Cornelius Warmerdam in 1957 with a rigid bamboo pole. In time young athletes from around the world followed suit and in no time at all, fibreglass poles displaced bamboo poles as the medium of choice. Interestingly, Wertsch notes that old timers, whose technique depended on bamboo poles, claimed that the rules of the game had fundamentally changed. Indeed, a few claimed that pole-vaulting was no longer the same sport and retired. Significantly, the analogy illustrates that the new mediational means (i.e. fibreglass poles) did not cause change in itself. Rather, change was driven from the bottom up as young vaulters from around the worlds started to exploit the affordances of a new medium to gain an edge in a competitive Olympic sport.

This provides a model for thinking about the drivers of cultural change in higher education. Indeed, it suggests that cultural change is not driven from the top down as the result of decisions taken by policymakers and university managers. Far from it, this sociocultural way of thinking suggests that change is driven from the bottom up by as students start to explore ways to exploit digital tools to gain an edge, become increasingly autonomous and take control over their own self-directed learning agendas. Significantly, digital tools and resources do not cause change; rather change is driven from the bottom up as advanced learners start to appropriate, experiment and discover new strategies and tactics that exploit their affordances.

Identity as a mediator and motivator of learning activity

The examples presented also start to suggest a need to understand learners' identities as powerful mediators and motivators of learning activity. Anastasia's resourcefulness cannot be understood without taking into account her commitment to becoming a social scientist capable of using advanced statistical analysis procedures. Similarly, Ardash's use of Amazon.com cannot be understood without taking into consideration his commitment to use his time at Oxford to broaden his mind. Indeed, if creative appropriations help learners address authentic learning needs, these needs often appear related to their commitments to a set of personal ethics or values which in turn appear related to their commitment to a strong projective identity or imagined future self. The following vignette helps to clarify this point. It shows how a student's commitment to an ethic of self-sufficiency, which in turn appears related to a commitment to a certain conception of herself as an autonomous, independent young professional, mediates the way she appropriates a spell checking tool.

Vignette: Sue Ellen's misuse of a spell checker

Sue Ellen regarded herself as a 'good' speller although she had experienced problems with differences between English and American spelling conventions. Since starting her Master's course she had set her spell checker to UK English to help her identify Americanized spellings. When users make a mistake using MS Word a squiggly red line appears beneath the incorrect spelling. Users then select a correct spelling from a list of alternatives that appear in a drop down menu. Nevertheless, Sue Ellen did *not* use it in this manner. She argued that the use of drop down menu of alternative might prevent her from learning the correct version of the word. Instead, she adopted a somewhat atypical strategy. In her own words:

> What I tend to do instead of waiting for spell check to change it I just start backspacing and I automatically change it until it will not be underlined ... [pause whilst demonstrating] ... So it basically just alerts me to the fact that it's been misspelt then I go and change it myself ... I find that's the best way to use it, well at least it works for me.
>
> (Sue Ellen, MSc Evidence Based Social Work)

To be clear, rather than right clicking on the word, Sue Ellen placed her cursor in the text, deleted the Americanized version of the word and then attempted to type the English alternative. If after pressing the space bar at the end of word, the squiggly red line re-appeared she knew she had made an error. At this point, she deleted the text and tried again. She then repeated this process until the line no longer appeared. Used in this way, the tool forced her to internalize the correct version of the word. Thus, her restricted use of the spell checking tool might be regarded as a tactic designed to guard against the perceived threat of *inhibited internalization*. The self-imposition of the enabling constraint effectively transformed the spell checking tool from a cognitive crutch to a powerful assistive learning companion.

The example illustrates the irreconcilable tension implicit in the concept of appropriation, as conceived by Bakhtin (1981), within the digital domain. Sue Ellen used digital tools in ways not intended by the designer to serve her own purposes and priorities. The manner or style of the appropriation seemed inextricably related to her personal commitment and ethic of self-sufficiency, which in turn seemed related to commitment to becoming an independent autonomous learner. Indeed, the vignette shows how a learners' commitment to a particular projective identity, conceived as a powerful mediator and motivator of learning activity shapes her use of the tool.

When we start to explore how resourceful individuals are exploiting new media to advance self-directed learning agendas (i.e. learning agendas not directed towards formal accreditation), the role of a projective identity as a powerful mediator and motivator of learning activity becomes even more conspicuous. The following two vignettes expand and develop this point.

Vignette: Clinton developing an independent critical perspective of political speeches using C-SPAN video podcasts

Clinton had a firm conviction that he was destined for a career in politics and was deeply committed to educating himself in preparation for this envisaged career trajectory. He had always read multiple newspapers on a daily basis. However, during his first year at Oxford he started to read multiple online newspapers throughout the day. Indeed, he argued that access to multiple online news sources helped him gain a more complex understanding of a particular issue from multiple perspectives.

> With so many resources at your fingertips, you are able to read the perspectives of many persuasions and I'm interested in policy and politics and culture ... and so for someone like me it's very important for me to learn about perspectives that are not my own and to do that I read different sources of news from different parts of the world maintained by organizations and individuals with different agendas.
>
> (Clinton, MSc Social Policy)

He was particularly keen on discerning representational bias in news reports relating to major political speeches. To this end, he read a variety of online news articles that reported the speech and then watched the raw video footage of the same speech on C-SPAN. This tactic allowed him to compare the different interpretations offered by different news sources and tease out the representational bias in each report. He was excited about the innovation of this new strategy. Discussing the tactic he stressed:

> ...you can watch the events and then read the coverage about them and see the bias very easily ... even more so than if you are comparing different news sources ... what I do now is watch the major policy speeches and the committee hearings and even the general assembly and I watched Tony Blair's questions for the press and Prime Minister's question time. I watch these things. Then you can see amazing discrepancies in what you have just read and how it's reported. That opens my eyes more than just the comparative new readings ... actually watching the events and reading transcripts of events.
>
> (Clinton, MSc Social Policy)

As a result, Clinton claimed that his stance on a number of policy issues had shifted. For example, when discussing his opposition to the war on Iraq he argued:

> I've learnt more about the war in Iraq. I read what everybody in the world is saying about it. Not just leaders and governors but citizens. I'm learning what their views are and why they are learning certain things. My opposition to the war on Iraq has grown stronger in reading the news sources from different parts of the United States and different parts of the world and the different kinds of reports I see on C-SPAN...
>
> (Clinton, MSc Social Policy)

The vignette suggests that, not unlike Ardash's use of Amazon.com for developing an insight into the 'webs of influence' between authors in inter-related fields, Clinton creatively appropriated multiple digital tools to develop a more in-depth understanding of a range of political and current affairs issues. Significantly, this act of creative appropriation did not simply lead to efficiency gains, it helped him gain different perspectives and thereby expand his conceptual understanding of a range of complex policy issues. The vignette also draws attention to the way a student's commitment to a strong projective identity motivated his innovative use of the web-based news media. Indeed, one cannot understand why Clinton invested so much time and energy into developing this technique without taking into con-sideration his deep commitment to a strong projective identity. In many respects he worked upon this identity as he engaged in these activities, at the same time it motivated his engagement with politics. In activity theo-retical terms it provided the 'object-motive' of this learning activity. The same pattern was evident in Jim's practice. The following vignette illustrates how Jim's use of Wikipedia as a tool to work upon his projective identity.

Vignette: Jim learns about the history of the British legal system using Wikipedia

Jim had a distinctively North American accent. He considered himself an outsider when it came to the British legal establishment. Moreover, he felt concerned that his sketchy knowledge of the history, traditions and institu-tions of the English legal system might show him up. Nevertheless the Inter-net provided him with access to resources that he could use to address these gaps in his knowledge. When interviewed he described how he spent an evening Googling in order to brush up on his understanding of the institu-tions that characterized the English legal system. For example, upon Goog-ling 'House of Lords' and 'Lord Chancellor', he discovered a Wikipedia article on Baron Woolf, Lord Chief Justice at the time.

This was the first time Jim had come across Wikipedia. Nevertheless, he immediately started to explore its potential as a learning resource and searched for other topics of interest. An interview transcript conveys Jim's initial discovery, enthusiasm and rapidly evolving use of the tool.

RF: What kind of things have you used it for?

JIM: umm ... a few things, general things. Like, I don't know about this subject or I want to know where such and such a person lived, like William Pitt and bang it comes up on Wikipedia and then I discover that there's a detailed article about his life.

RF: So what do you think of it?

JIM: How do I like it? I think it's terrific! I love the idea ... I like it for its utility, the spirit of the idea to provide free information ... and the idea that all of these people acting independently can get together and produce such an enormous and high quality volume of information that will someday end up being one of the most comprehensive sources of information because they are just hyperlinking more and more and more stuff. And this is just the beginning. I really think that in five years you'll have almost everything up there. I don't know how quality control will be managed in the end but it seems to be pretty well run so far.

RF: So can you just take me through a few examples of what you were looking for?

JIM: Yep, the Lord Chancellor's Office, it had the history, the background, what functions they have, their responsibilities ... The other thing, I wanted to know about the court structure in Britain, so I typed in 'Queen's Bench' or something. Because the way the court system has evolved is very organic and piecemeal – as opposed to one person's idea of what the courts should be ... erm and so it's tricky knowing what's what with constitutional reform in Britain. Incidentally, I was looking at the House of Lords and I wanted to know what the reform proposals were – they were planning to abolish the judicial committee in the House of Lords and establish a supreme court. Well they are not prepared they've actually passed the act to create a supreme court.

RF: Really?

(Jim, MSt Law)

The vignette illustrates a student in the process of buying into the ethic of participatory culture; a culture that one might at once take from and contribute to. At the same time, it illustrates an awareness of the new challenges and choices participation might entail. Indeed, it is interesting to note how quickly Jim became committed to the 'spirit of the idea' but remained slightly concerned about 'quality control'. Further, it sensitizes us to the utility of user generated content as resource for learners and hints at the opportunities for incidental learning that follow from an initial search. However, most significantly, it suggests how this particular creative appropriation is mediated and motivated by Jim's commitment to becoming a fully fledged member of the British legal establishment. Like Clinton, Jim creatively appropriates a newly discovered tool to take control of a self-directed learning trajectory motivated by a commitment to a strong projective identity. This theme is revisited and developed in Chapter 6. For now it is important to understand that we cannot account for some of the surprising and unexpected ways students appropriated new media beyond the confines of particular courses of study without taking into account their commitment to become certain kinds of persons.

Challenges, choices and new media literacies

This chapter draws attention to some of creative and unexpected ways university students are now creatively appropriating web-based tools to address authentic learning needs. These vignettes suggest all sorts of new opportunities and sensitize us to some of the associated new media literacies. Nevertheless, they also highlight some of the challenges and choices confronting students as they venture into participatory cultures.

The anxiety of choice

Media change continues unabated confronting users with additional challenges and choices as new tools, with overlapping functionalities, become available. With increasingly powerful search tools, students are not entirely alone when attempting to find quality web-based instructional material. Nevertheless, they remain responsible for evaluating and categorizing the utility of each resource for their specific purposes. A single Google search might return links to materials provided by universities, materials provided by commercial services or charitable organizations or user generated content uploaded by another academics and students on personal blogs. Students are then compelled to take on the onus of responsibility for assessing the quality of online resources and filtering the information they confront. This problem becomes particularly astute given the increasingly volumes of user generated content on the Internet. Students can no longer rely on the editors, teachers, tutors and publishing houses to filter the information available in the public domain. They must choose, and invariably choose alone.

Learning in a space governed by the laws of attention economics

The competing demands made on students' attention as they attempt to negotiate personalized learning trajectories through this emergent media landscape compound this anxiety of choice. According to Goldhaber (1996) attention is the one scare commodity in cyberspace and since all economies evolve around scare resources the primary challenge confronting online commercial ventures is to capture and retain the attention of potential customers. According to this theory all the highly successful online businesses (i.e. Amazon, Facebook, My Space, Google and YouTube) have succeeded as commercial ventures precisely because they have innovated successful strategies for capturing and retaining users' attention. In short, cyberspace is subject to the laws of attention economics.

This theory was developed to understand and conceptualize the challenges confronting businesses attempting to monopolize new marketing opportunities. However, it also draws attention to some of the new challenges and choices confronting learners as they struggle to self-regulate their own attention. For example, Anastasia was exposed to countless links to online book stores attempting to sell statistics textbooks as she searched for useful free learning materials. In short, sponsored and unsponsored links with commercial agendas all compete for the attention of the learner as they seek out new tools and resources to address authentic learning needs. As a result, students are compelled to develop counter tactics to resist attempts to usurp their agency.

This invariably involves an internalized commitment. Ardash's commitment to using Amazon.com, not simply to buy books, but as a tool to find out more about a particularly book before 'wasting time' going to the library constitutes an internalized commitment to resist a commercial agenda as did Sue Ellen's commitment to working on the college computer which was 'free of distractions' and Katrina's commitment to leaving her Ethernet cable at home when she headed to the library. Indeed, multiple examples suggest that university students must now learn to resist an increasing variety of sophisticated strategies that are designed to recruit their attention if they are to make effective use of the Internet as a learning resource.

Anticipating the relative advantages of adoption

Finally, students are confronted with choices when anticipating the relative advantages and drawbacks of adopting a new tool. Students have the option of using a variety of purposefully designed research tools, such as Wikipedia and the Oxford English Dictionary online, in combination with traditional tools and resources. Nevertheless, a capacity to forecast the implications of adopting a particular tool and using it in combination with traditional resources poses additional challenges. Sue Ellen's decision not to use Endnote as a reference manager provides an interesting example in which the agency of the learner becomes conspicuous.

Vignette: Sue Ellen rejects Endnote

Sue Ellen started to use Endnote because most of the students on her course had started to use it. She recognized the potential advantages of using a reference manager. However, her initial experience of using the tool appeared to disrupt her internalized commitment to an ethic of self sufficiency. The following extract suggests how this internalize commitment mediated her thought processes as she forecasted the implications of adoption.

SE: Here's an account of my basic exploration of Endnote. I basically doubled clicked, look at it, read the basic instructions about how to use it and then I thought fuck it, I'll just compile the bibliography on my own.

RF: So there wasn't a tangible enough advantage to be gained?

SE: No. Because the time it would take me to learn how to use it and then format and ... you'd still have to punch all the information into Endnote...

RF: Did you know you can connect to databases and stuff?

SE: Yes but that sound complicated as well, plus the style that they want you to use is slightly off from the ones I need to use ... and it's kind of off by parentheses and stuff like that so that would mean I'd need to go in there and tidy it all up and I think I might as well just do it myself.

(Sue Ellen, MSc Evidence Based Social Work)

The vignette illustrates a student forecasting the relative advantages and potential drawbacks of adoption. In this instance she estimates adoption would create additional work. Further, the phrase, 'the style they want you to use', suggests that she regarded the intentions of the toolmakers, now designed into the tool, as a threat to her own autonomy. In addition, it suggests that she anticipated that adoption would diminish her control over the reference managing process.

The agency of learners is revealed in acts of resistance. Nevertheless, adoption is not always a matter of personal preference. Individuals may find themselves under considerable social pressure to adopt. Technology refusers may find themselves at a significant disadvantage when venture into the work place and may lose out on opportunities for tactical redeployments.

Summary

As a theoretical lens, the notion of creative appropriation directs our attention to some of the surprising and unexpected ways students are now using digital media to expand learning opportunities and take control over their own learning agendas. Some of the examples used to illustrate this processes might seem ingenious, some might appear trivial. On one level, they suggest some of the playful, creative, exploratory and inventive ways university students are gaining an edge with new media. However, these examples also serve to illustrate how creative appropriations at a microgenetic level have started to drive a process of cultural transition from the bottom up. Moreover, in a time of rapid media change, they suggest the pressures on students to continually innovate and adapt in order to remain competitive. More holistically, this chapter suggests why we need to understand creative appropriation, like design, as a fundamental aspect of new media literacy. Finally, it suggests that learners who are successfully negotiating the challenges and choices they are confronted with as they start to use digital media as their primary learning resources have invariably internalized a commitment to a strong projective identity.

5 Globally distributed funds of living knowledge

> The digital information technology is important for learning and education, not primarily because it offers a mechanism to transfer pre-packed information. That is a too one-dimensional perspective. Its consequences touch on more basic displacements in the ways in which knowledge is produced and mediated. It contributes to the creation of new arenas to communicate in, and new virtual contexts to develop in.
>
> (Säljö 2004: 227)

> Our living knowledge, skills, and abilities are in the process of being recognized as the primary source of all other wealth. What then will our new communication tools be used for? The most socially useful goal will no doubt be to supply ourselves with the instruments for sharing our mental abilities in the construction of collective intellect or imagination.
>
> (Lévy 1997: 9)

Introduction

Few would object to Lévy's (1997) utopian and humanistic vision of a world in which a new generation of tools provide the technical infrastructure that allows the dynamic sharing of collective intelligence amongst distributed communities for mutual advantage. However, much of the existing research within the field of Computer Supported Collaborative Learning (CSCL) suggests that many learners are not so quick to engage, share knowledge and learn collaboratively with others through new media. Crook and Light (2002: 171) note that electronic seminar spaces, set up by university computer services to support taught courses, remained unused by over 90 per cent of course tutors. Of the remaining 10 per cent that were used, the online discussion was dominated by a small number of individuals. They highlight: (a) the breakdown in the turn-taking protocols associated with face-to-face group discussion; (b) the very measured style of participation attributed to the fact that posts remained open to inspection; and (c) the 'abrasive, irrelevance, and irreverence' that welled up when no moderator was present. Muukkonen *et al.* (2005: 535) highlight the 'interrelated difficulties' that arise when tutors attempt to integrate online discussion forums into structured courses. Recurrent themes include: problems with intensity of participation, shortness of discourse threads and lack of reciprocity. Kreijns, Kischner and Jochems (2003) stress that many tutors erroneously take it for granted that participants will socially interact simply because it is possible. Moreover, their metareview of the CSCL literature stresses that a sole focus on cognitive processes in instructional activities neglects the social, cultural and economic circumstances that impact on students' participation.

What appears to be missing from the literature is an understanding of how learners, left to their own devices, actively appropriate social media to leverage expertise of others within and across institutional boundaries. Nardi argues:

> Paradoxically, we find that the most fundamental unit of analysis for computer-supported cooperative work is not at the group level for many tasks and settings, but at the individual level as personal social networks come to be more and more important. Collectively subjects are increasingly put together through the assemblage of people found through personal networks rather than being constituted as teams created through organizational planning and structuring. Teams are still important but they are not the centrepiece of labour management they once were, nor are they the chief resource for individual workers.
>
> (Nardi *et al.* 2002: 205)

Her theorizing is grounded ethnographic work that explores how professionals create, build and nurture personal networks and then activate subnetworks of individuals when need arises to work on specific problems. In this respect, it is interesting to consider how students, the young professionals of tomorrow, start to build, nurture and activate extended personal networks whilst at university to achieve these purposes (study-related and otherwise) prior to the jump into the job market.

The following chapter attempts to redress the imbalance that has arisen as a result of a preoccupation with collaborative spaces purposefully established by course tutors to support learning. It attempts to shift the focus of attention towards an emergent and possibly far more significant arena of informal learning activity afforded by what Säljö (2004: 227) describes as 'more basic displacements in the ways in which knowledge is produced and mediated'.

The vignettes introduced in this chapter illustrate how informal personal networks emerge from the lifeworld of everyday college life, how these networks are nurtured over time and how sub-networks and individuals are then activated to address learning needs as they arise. Sociocultural and activity theory equips us with some powerful conceptual tools that help us understand this process.

Conceptual building blocks for understanding collaborative learning beyond the networked university

Moll *et al.* (1992, 1997) use the term 'funds of living knowledge' to suggest how an extended family operates as a living system of shared knowledge and expertise. The research team conducted a cognitive anthropology of learning in and out of schools in Mexican working class communities in Tucson, Arizona. Their research suggests how the exchange of knowledge, skills and labour essential for a family's functioning and collective well-being are inter-connected through the 'household'. Indeed, the 'household' mediates the formation of a 'living system of knowledge' (Moll *et al.* 1997: 140).

Each family studied had developed strategies and arrangements that facilitated the exchange of 'funds of knowledge'. Interestingly, the comparison with classrooms, in which access to living 'funds of knowledge' is relatively restricted, reveals that 'the social environment does not take a neutral view towards the acquisition of knowledge and skill, but is instead highly interested, and often directive, controlling or even denying access to information' (op. cit.: 260). The concept provides a powerful tool for understanding the exchange of knowledge and expertise mediated by social software tools.

There remains, however, a need for tools that focus attention on the ways individuals exploit and leverage the knowledge and expertise accessible through their funds of knowledge. Rogoff (1990) stresses the active role played by learners in recruiting the assistance of more capable peers. The notion of 'intent participation' identifies a genre of practice in which 'children are active in directing the support of adults and the adjustment of that support as their skills develop' (p. 106). In contrast to the dominant metaphor of *scaffolding* (Wood *et al.* 1976), 'intent participation' suggests how toddlers actively manage the assistance of their caregivers adjusting the level of assistance and guidance provided if and when required. It is interesting to consider how students intently participate in online spaces and actively manage the assistance of remote learning companions. This is particularly important given that much of the scaffolding associated with traditional learning environments is conspicuously absent. Nevertheless, whilst useful, the notion of 'intent participation' remains ill-defined and tends to assume a significant age and skill gap between the learner and the tutor, a differential that is rarely so pronounced or significant among groups of graduate students.

Edwards (2005; Edwards and D'Arcy 2004) is developing the concept of 'relational agency' for understanding how active, agentive individuals recruit and manage the assistance of others within and across institutional boundaries. Relational agency is defined as a 'capacity which involves recognizing that another person may be a resource and that work needs to be done to elicit, recognize and negotiate the use of that resource in order to align oneself in joint action on the object' (Edwards 2005: 172). The concept is offered as a conceptual tool for understanding informal modes of collaboration among professionals in workplace and educational settings. Edwards argues:

Relational agency is not simply a matter of collaborative action on an object. Rather it is a capacity to recognize and use the support of others in order to transform the object. It is an ability to seek out and use others as resources for action and equally to be able to respond to the need for support from others. Relational agency is therefore based on a fluid and open-ended notion of the ZPD.

(Edwards and D'Arcy 2004: 149)

Referring to the findings of empirical research focused on the practices of professionals working across organization boundaries, she adds:

In our analyses of evidence from the studies, we are working with the idea of the ZPD as a set of interactions which is on-going in a social setting i.e. not simply a contrived interaction aimed at achieving one learning outcome.

(ibid.)

Significantly, the concept of relational agency does not describe a particular kind of personal network, or community of practice so much as the 'micro-relations' between learners in open ended learning zones. Indeed, Edwards claims that the concept enables us to better understand how individuals might reach out and connect with others to create a mutual (sometimes fleeting) zone of proximal development that enables both parties to achieve more than they would be capable of achieving unassisted. Moreover, it is recognized as an expert-like capacity to work across the 'mobile and dislocated communities of late capitalism' in which 'individuals are connected as never before', creating 'paradoxical intentions' for those who inhabit transient communities, which consequently put a 'strain on a sense of self' (Edwards 2005: 169). In this respect, relational agency is conceived as a capacity of an individual to seek synergistic personal relationships across multiple interconnected networks, contexts and activity systems.

The formation of a fund of living knowledge

The concept of 'funds of knowledge' and 'relational agency' are particularly useful for understanding collaborative working practices mediated by social software tools. The following vignettes tell a story. By assembling fragments from various localized insider perspectives into a narrative accounts, they attempt to suggest how students: a) appropriate simple CMC (computer mediated communications) tools (like e-mail) to build and sustain a fund of living knowledge; b) nurture and maintain a fund of living knowledge through seemingly trivial nurturing practices such as the posting of away messages; and c) mobilize or activate the distributed expertise accessible through a globally distributed fund of living knowledge to address authentic learning needs.

Vignette: Daisy cultivating and mobilizing a fund of living knowledge

It is common for students studying masters' courses with heavy reading loads to form study groups in preparation for exams. Study groups allow students to divide the workload required, revise topics, assimilate notes and facilitate the assimilation of knowledge through collective discussion. Both Daisy and Katrina had participated in informal study groups that students organized to prepare themselves for exams.

The group started when Daisy and two other course mates met over lunch and agreed to meet once a week to share notes and discuss topics in preparation for the exams. Daisy then asked two others to join the group: a male friend (who she persuaded to defect from a rival study group) and another female friend who, she argued, 'could provide different perspectives' because she had followed a slightly different reading list with a different supervisor. After a series of informal face-to-face discussions, Daisy activated the network with a group e-mail:

> Hello gang!
>
> Exams are on their way (boo!) so let's get together and work out our strategy! The sooner the better I think. I will be in London tomorrow but how about Tuesday? I assume we will all be at the lecture at 12 and Jake, I know you have your option from 3 onwards so let's meet at 10:30 at ISCA? That would give us an hour and a bit to chat and figure out what we are going to focus on and how we will divide the work. Maybe it would be good to bring reading lists, etc.? Let us know if you have any better suggestions re: time/location...
>
> See you Tuesday otherwise,

She then convened an initial meeting where members drew up a list of essential and non-essential topics to cover. Each student then went away and prepared notes. These were later shared with other members of the group. Individuals were responsible for photocopying notes to facilitate face-to-face discussion at each meeting and e-mailing group members a copy of the notes they had made. Most of the articles were directly available on AnthroSource, an online service that acted as a portal for the top anthropology journals and integrated access to older articles on JSTOR, a free electronic archive of old journal articles. A few articles were not available online but Daisy argued, 'if it's not online I won't bother to read it'.

In addition to the sharing of articles, the group e-mail allowed members to post queries such as, 'has any one read Kusserow on individualism?', or request specific assistance. Daisy felt she was often the target of such requests, such as the one made by Jake.

> Hey, D: I remember you saying how much you liked this topic – would I be able to take a look at your essay on this one? Sorry for bugging you so much...!
>   xo, Jake

However, it also enabled her to receive critical or supportive feedback from those who read her essays.

> hi Daisy,
> just read your essay on gender in west africa. it's a good essay, i think, and it was useful to me to supplement my readings on gender (basically piot and ferme). Thanks for sending it. and good luck with your last week's of preparation!
> best dean

She estimated between ten and fifteen postings on the list would be made in between weekly meetings. However, initially at least, she argued that she had to 'drive' the process.

> Hello everyone!
> Am sending more revision notes but not sure who has what or what you need ... Also, Daniel and I are meeting Friday 10 am to go through some exam questions and try to come up with ideas about outlines ... you are all welcome! Hope studying is going well ... what a gorgeous day!
> Love,
> D

As suggested, Daisy also sent out regular updates describing what she had done (including current notes) and encouraged others to do the same. She argued that this helped to 'speed things up'. Indeed, this strategy appeared to motivate others and, in a reciprocal manner, motivate Daisy.

When sharing personal essays, students also included comments relating to feedback they had received from their supervisor. This strategy appeared to feed knowledge acquired through private conversations into the collective learning process. For example, a student named Susan posted the following comment:

> Hi guys! Sorry for being so absent from everything I've had a few things going on other than studying. Here is my colonial essay though. Beth said: super essay! Thoughtful balanced and well argued. You could take a broader perspective and think about power or colonialism in a very particular or historically bounded version of wider power relations.

This sharing of information created a sense that the group was progressing and becoming more sensitized to the strengths and weaknesses of particular essays.

This vignette draws attention to the way a simple group e-mail mediated the formation of a 'fund of living knowledge', which grew out of day-to-day conversations and informal collaboration between members of a very personal network of students, based in the same academic department, who referred to themselves as 'friends'. Nevertheless, the successful operation of this group appeared to depend upon an individual's capacity for relational agency. Daisy pulled in additional human resources into a collective group activity, she allowed for the fact that not all contributed to the same degree and took an active role in sustaining the momentum of the group. For her, at least, the bonding and camaraderie among course mates was as important as the produc- tivity gains achieved through the division of labour. Indeed, the posting of regular updates appeared to create a sense of commitment to a collective group activity. In short, whilst discussion (focused on the article summaries) took place at the face-to-face meetings, the flow of daily messages helped to create a sense that the group was making steady progress towards a common objective. Indeed, Daisy repeatedly stressed that the activity 'bought the group together'. This had a motivating effect and helped to bolster their sense of purpose and commitment to the task at hand.

It is important to emphasize that group e-mails did not displace the prac- tice of learning through informal face-to-face discussion. This was not an online community. However, the group e-mail afforded additional exchanges of knowledge and expertise that continued between face-to-face meetings. Further, it is important to stress that this activity system remained orien- tated on a very concrete objective (i.e. the need to prepare for the forthcom- ing exam) which motivated the formation of this informal learning community.

Cultivating and nurturing globally distributed funds of living knowledge

Engagement in a shared activity, such as an informal study group, provides an arena in which intellectual relationships between learning companions are formed. Daisy's story hints at the way a shared object (i.e. an exam) might lead to the formation of a fund of living knowledge. However, it does not suggest the way social media might allow individuals to nurture a fund of living knowledge over time. Edina, Sue Ellen and Miss Lullaby's use of social software tools revealed a far less object-orientated form of activity that appeared motivated by a need to remain connected with an extended per- sonal network after the conditions that led to their original formation no longer existed. In addition, their use of social software tools illustrates a range of nurturing strategies that appeared important as a mechanism for sustaining the social, personal and affective bounds that existed between group members.

Vignette: Miss Lullaby working with MSN Messenger always-on

Miss Lullaby worked with her MSN Messenger always-on. She argued that an always-on connection to course mates through a 'buddy list' entitled 'Uno Folkitos' provided a form of 'emotional support'. For example, whilst demon- strating the use of the tool she remarked:

> ...when I'm in the middle of working and I'm feeling frustrated I can just IM someone and say look, 'how's it going for you?' and they'll say, 'I have so many words but having a hard time with this'. Then I realize that it's not me doing something incorrectly, it's just part of the process.
>
> (Miss Lullaby, MSc Social Policy)

In short, the tool was not used to discuss academic work directly, but used to create a supportive quasi-virtual context when working alone in her study room. However, it could be used to gauge progress on a particular task. For example, she remarked:

> Like right now we're working on our dissertations and you know, I'll say 'how much work are you getting done each day? How many sources are you using? Are you quoting?' You know really general stuff.

She was not in direct contact with everyone on her taught course through the tool. Indeed, she now only exchanged instant messages with three others who had now become 'close friends'. Interestingly she stressed that these three course mates already had MSN Messenger accounts. When they met, the tool came up in conversation and they exchanged MSN screen names. In short, the tool didn't create new friendships. However, it afforded new opportunities for these relationships to develop within the virtual sphere. She stressed, 'I wouldn't have that sort of conversation with somebody who I wasn't beginning to get close to in the first place'. She added, it 'helps us have friendships', 'it helps the normal feel of a friendship' and suggested 'it increases the solidarity that we feel with each other'. In short, the tool enabled her to bond closely with people with whom she felt inclined to bond.

At a surface level it would seem that the tool was used wholly for social purposes. Nevertheless, this would underestimate the ways it started to provide emotive and motivational support. Interestingly, when asked, 'Do you think it has actually improved the quality of your work?' Miss Lullaby replied, 'Well, I think it does because it gives me confidence ... it helps to know that other people are having the same issues that I'm experiencing'. Not unlike the e-mail list serve used by Daisy and her course mates, the tool help to create a sense of shared endeavour. However, unlike the e-mail list serve MSN Messenger remained 'always-on' and therefore created a permanent sense of co-presence.

Unlike Miss Lullaby, Edina no longer required a tool to support her through a period of study. However, MSN Messenger remained an important tool for sustaining a sense of community with course mates who had started to disperse. It enabled her to stay virtually connected people she no longer saw face-to-face on a regular basis. Her story is important for understanding how this community may have started to function as 'fund of living knowledge' that might be exploited by group members as a learning resource for the years to come.

Edina was in contact with most of her course mates through MSN Messenger. She liked the way it enabled her to monitor what people were doing. This was *not* achieved through the exchange of instant messages. Indeed, she chose to 'skulk' most of the time. In other words, she adjusted the privacy settings on MSN Messenger so as to appear offline or busy. This allowed her to monitor the posts and online status of others (including their 'away messages') whilst appearing to be offline and avoid distractions. However, the posting of away messages (visible to all members of her 'buddy list') allowed 'buddies' to suggest what they were doing at a particular point in time. Edina argued, 'It's also a good way of sending a message to everyone to let them know about the general lie of the land at your end'.

Edina changed her 'away message' everyday. When interviewed her away message read: 'Flowers for everyone'. She explained she had been feeling 'expansive and generous' that day and laughed. However, the message was frequently changed to reflect her changing mood and circumstances. She explained:

> When I was writing my dissertation I could just write one line explaining how I felt about things. One day I'd be 'Refugees traumatize me' because I was studying psychosocial trauma for refugees. Another day I'd be 'Send 'em back!' which was a kind of joke. But we all call each other different things. When we finished our dissertations I was, 'It's over thank God!'
>
> (Edina, MSc Forced Migration)

During the course of the stimulated response, she decided to change her away name to 'Forced to Migrate' because she was being 'kicked out of her room' at the end of the month. The play on words connoted her field of academic inquiry but also signified that her personal predicament and concern about finding somewhere else to live. In short, she used the 'away message' to broadcast her changing circumstances and mood to a community who had been very much part of her everyday life. However, Edina now used the tool to monitor the movements, moods and activities of this community as they dispersed around the world.

Significantly, many of Edina's course mates were also starting to look for jobs. Whilst the routines and rituals associated with her master's course played an important role in mediating the formation of this fund of knowledge, MSN Messenger had taken on a new function as a mediator of what was rapidly becoming a globally distributed fund of living knowledge. Talking me through her 'buddy list', Edina pointed at the screen and provided a short commentary on the movements of this group:

> ...he's in Birmingham, he's in France, she's in Spain, she's in Canada, she's in Lebanon, he's in Canada, she's in Lebanon, he's in Reading, he's in Oxford, she's in Canada ... her – I have no idea – I haven't seen her online for several years now.
>
> [RF interrupts] – Why does it say, 'I am King Kong's Banana!'
>
> [Edina responds] yes he always puts up these funny away messages. Yes, he's in Greece.
>
> (Edina, MSc Forced Migration)

> The comment suggests that her course mates were now becoming part of a more widely distributed community that also included friends from former courses, friends from school and certain members of her extended family. Picking out a particular away message that read 'Refugee happy', she smiled and said, 'That's my friend, Alan. That means he's finished his exams.'

The vignette suggests that whilst tools like MSN Messenger might not support study or informal learning in a direct way, they do help to create and sustain a virtual social context conducive to study and help a dispersing community to remain connected. Whilst working on dissertation assignments, the tool helped to create a sense of community among course mates who were spending large parts of their day alone in their study rooms. Although the tool did not facilitate the exchange of information or critical feedback, it did function as a source of motivation and emotional support. Changing an 'away message' took seconds rather than minutes and was available for all to see. In this respect, the tool proved far more effective than e-mail or chat as a mode of communication. Further, the posting of away messages functioned as a highly efficient means of maintaining an extended personal network of loose ties as the group started to disperse. The wordplay and widespread use of humour, irony and caricature appeared quite normal within this mode of communicative practice. Indeed, it seemed important for bonding purposes.

The wordplay and humour should not eclipse the fact that the personal networks that form through seemingly trivial practices might become a powerful fund of living knowledge. Edina was seeking a job with a 'higher purpose' and was beginning to look for employment in the non-governmental organization (NGO) sector, a world where strong and loose ties with others seeking employment in the same field could become potentially a valuable resource. Indeed, Edina went on to work for the United Nations doing refugee determinations in sub-Saharan Africa and maintained regular contact with others on her course who took jobs around the world. In this respect, the case hints at the way in which a personal network might evolve into a fund of living knowledge. It does not, however, shed light on the process of mobilizing members of this distributed community. Edina had not yet started to mobilize others as a resource to advance her purposes.

Sue Ellen was more conscious of the potential advantages that might be gleaned from cultivating this network. She had migrated from MSN Messenger to Friendster. For the most part, her Friendster activities appeared wholly playful and social. The tool included a messenger service but also afforded the capacity to upload, share and tag photographs, write personal 'testimonials' about friends and send electronic gifts. She talked enthusiastically about the various ways she used these tools to nurture her personal network. However, she also suggested that she foresaw how this growing personal network might one day become a powerful resource for someone who was intending to return to the United States and work in public policy. Other students used different tools for much the same purpose. Whilst Katrina resisted using instant messenger or social software tools altogether, she periodically circulated an update of her life to a globally distributed network of friends using a group e-mail. In effect, she used the tool as a personal blog. This appeared to serve a similar one-to-many nurturing function akin to the posting of away messages. Clinton, who treated social networking as his training for public office, made extensive use of a 'birthday reminder' tool to nurture a bond with young democrats and politicos he had met from around the world.

Facebook mediates the formation of globally distributed funds of living knowledge among thousands of Oxford alumni. The social software platform was specifically designed to facilitate the maintenance of distributed communities of college graduates that supported multiple personal and 'just for fun' networks as special interest groups. One of the most interesting challenges for sociocultural researchers is to understand how these networks might actually benefit graduates in years to come. Conceived as part of a virtually figured world, these observations suggest that one of the most significant issues is how participation with these communities might help students maintain a strong projective identity and sustain an individual in a particular life trajectory. However, it also important to consider how and why an individual might exploit a globally distributed fund of living knowledge to address an authentic learning needs as they arise.

Mobilizing a globally distributed fund of living knowledge

The examples given only hint at some of the ways individuals might leverage the distributed expertise accessible within a well-nurtured fund of living knowledge. The following vignette illustrates how an individual exercises relational agency and mobilizes the distributed expertise available through a well nurtured globally distributed fund of living knowledge.

Vignette: Miss Lullaby activates a personal network of critical friends

Miss Lullaby had used a range of social tools for many years. Besides being an 'e-mail junkie', 'chat addict', and self-confessed 'cyber flirt', she was a fierce critic of the death penalty. She was on a social policy master's course with a view to researching and writing about the social implications of capital punishment.[1] Although confident when speaking about her academic interests, she confessed a lack of confidence in her written work, which she felt was often 'too wordy' and 'repetitive'. Nevertheless, over the years she had developed an extensive network of 'critical friends' who proofed and edited her work. This distributed network of critical friends had evolved since her undergraduate days at UCLA, and had now become integrated into her general writing strategy.

The success of this strategy depended a great deal on her ability to cultivate and nurture a fund of living knowledge consisting of over a dozen potential critical friends and reviewers. To gain specific critical feedback, editorial advice and assistance with proofreading, she typically requested help from friends from 'back home' in California. She knew what these friends were doing on a daily basis through browsing their away messages. Not unlike Edina, she nurtured her personal network by constant exchanges of away messages, photo tags and electronic gift exchanges. However, she actively recruited new recruits into her fund of living knowledge. Paul, a medical doctor, was a relatively new recruit she found 'exceptionally good' at providing critical scrutiny on her interpretation of data she had collected on the healthcare system. Building her network with specialists like Paul over time enabled her to spread the burden of requests and elicit particular kinds of specialist feedback if and when required.

She argued that she often learnt by studying the 'structure' and 'logic' of her friends' essays during the review process:

> I learn about different styles of writing of academic work. I think that you can become very accustomed to doing things in a particular way. And so it's good for me to see work in progress, and see what that progress is like ... and how someone is choosing to structure their paper. It's interesting to look at the logic behind papers sometimes.
>
> (Miss Lullaby, MSc Social Policy)

Over time, this process had helped her internalize the knowledge and expertise of her distributed community of learning companions.

Given her growing dependence on the expertise of particular people, a capacity to reciprocate became particularly important. She considered it a duty to provide a similar service to any of her critical friends. However, this created additional challenges and choices. On one level she felt 'honoured and privileged' when asked to review the work of a friend because it signified that they trusted her opinion. However, this made demands on her time.

She was concerned that she might become overly dependent on particular critical friends, but then suggested that this form of dependency had simply displaced a prior dependence on a centralized service.

> Well actually, I'm becoming less dependent because I don't seek help as much as I did before. At my university, my undergraduate university, there was a thing called the writing centre and you could make appointments with professors who would look over your work. It could be a letter. It could be a huge paper. I would make appointments; I would have an hour consultation about my work. It was easy to get access to professional proofreaders basically. But here, because there is no such facility, I feel like I'm not typical in asking for assistance, I'm almost embarrassed to ask for help from my course mates here. Because they wonder what it is that I'm so nervous about.
>
> (Miss Lullaby, MSc Social Policy)

In this respect, access to social media allowed her to become less dependent on a particular writing centre and develop a distributed fund of reviewers and proofreaders that she managed actively and controlled. In the process, the burden of responsibility for supporting written assignments had shifted from the writing centre to this self-regulated and self-managed distributed globally distributed fund of knowledge; a fund of living knowledge that she took with her as she moved across institutional contexts and had thereby started to support a lifelong learning agenda.

On one occasion, shortly after interview, Miss Lullaby found herself in a double bind. She was the final stages of completing her master's dissertation with a submission deadline looming. Her academic supervisor was overseas and had not responded to several e-mail requests for help. Rather than despair about the inadequacy of the supervision she was receiving, she turned to her distributed fund of living knowledge for help. She identified two people within her personal network as potential resources who possessed the necessary knowledge and skills to assist: a 'subject specialist' – whom she knew from her undergraduate days – and a 'non-specialist' to provide a more general feedback on the style and language use. Both had agreed to assist. She summarized her rationale thus:

> I've got two people who are going to look at it for me. One who is a specialist in the field and one who doesn't know anything about it. He's just going to look at it as well. It's sometimes good to have someone who doesn't really know the field so they can look at it and question whether you are really explaining things well enough. So that someone who is a novice can pick it up and really understand your argument. So I really like it when someone reads a paper of mine before I submit it who doesn't have any experience with the topic at all.
>
> (Miss Lullaby, MSc Social Policy)

Both reviewers also agreed to use the track changes facility in MS Word. She had used this tool routinely for a number of years. In general, she felt that this encouraged reviewers to provide more specific and detailed feedback. Moreover, she liked the option of either rejecting or accepting the changes with a click of the mouse. In her estimation, by asking her critical friends to use the tool she was increasing the probability of receiving focused and detailed feedback. This, in turn, would reduce the time it would take her to make the corrections.

The vignette illustrates an advanced learner with an extremely well-cultivated globally distributed fund of living knowledge activating the distributed expertise of individuals to help her escape a double bind. Her practice was not typical. Miss Lullaby had some specific learning needs and had invested years developing strategies that might enable her to address these needs. Nevertheless, other students demonstrated a capacity to exercise relational agency and mobilize their distributed funds of living knowledge in a variety of ways.

ZeroGBoy maintained daily contact with his mother. As a working academic, she understood the higher education employment market and was able to provide valuable advice and guidance as he started to apply for jobs. Compared to senior members of the department in which ZeroGBoy had studied, her advice remained impartial. Clinton maintained a close link with the former president of his undergraduate university with whom he consulted when attempting to make important career decisions. Over time this relationship had evolved into an informal lifelong mentorship nurtured and maintained through regular exchanges. Similarly, Anastasia remained in regular contact with her former supervisor in Romania through regular e-mail exchanges and regularly drew upon her knowledge and experience as a resource.

Nurturing a globally distributed fund of living knowledge

In previously decades the telephone afforded individuals opportunities to cultivate a distributed fund of living knowledge. However, this came at a price. Today always-on connectivity, in combination with e-mail, chat and free Internet telephony, affords students new opportunities to nurture, maintain and activate funds of living knowledge wherever they might be at a negligible cost any time of day or night. Thus, it seems likely that this emergent genre of informal learning activity is set to become more significant in students' everyday lives. However, it is important to emphasize that it requires work to cultivate, maintain and nurture a fund of living knowledge. The interactions described in this chapter were not necessarily ongoing. Indeed, the funds of knowledge students draw upon as a resource might remain dormant for long periods of time before being mobilized to address a particular learning need (i.e. proofreading, critical feedback or finding a job). Nevertheless, it seems that social software affords students new opportunities to nurture globally distributed funds of living knowledge. Indeed, most of these interactions grew out of ongoing participation in a virtual social settings mediated by social software tools. This is not dissimilar to the way that Moll *et al.*'s funds of living knowledge were sustained by day-to-day rituals mediated by the 'household' in the everyday lives of Mexican working class families. Indeed, conceived as a mediator that fostered emotional bonds and a sense of obligation among globally distributed personal networks social software applications like MSN Messenger and Facebook appear to function in like a Moll *et al.*'s 'household'. Both mediated bonds between members of tightly knit personal networks and fostered a sense of obligation among students to assist one another when need arose.

This way of thinking about collaborative working relationship draws one's attention to the importance of nurturing practices. Indeed, the cultivation and maintenance of a globally distributed fund of living knowledge involves requires work. Further, an individual's capacity to draw upon the expertise of others may depend heavily on prior nurturing activity. Interestingly, Miss Lullaby reported making demands on one former classmate, despite that her friend 'hated' editing her work. The bond or obligation that existed between Miss Lullaby and her friend appeared to resemble the kind of obligations that exist between the members of an extended family. These bonds had developed over years through shared experiences and social interactions on- and offline. From this perspective, it is misleading to think of a globally distributed fund of knowledge as an *online* learning community. Indeed, it suggests that globally distributed funds of living knowledge are forged through shared lifeworld experiences: taking courses; preparing for exams; graduating together; and going to college parties. Nevertheless, it also highlights the way social software, unlike Moll *et al.*'s 'household', empowers learners to maintain close personal bounds with others as they move across institutional boundaries.

For many students personal networks supported by tools like MSN Messenger consisted of heterogeneous groups from multiple lifeworld communities, past and present. In turn, these observations highlight the significance of what on the surface might seem like rather trivial and playful practices. From a sociocultural perspective the posting of humorous away messages, the sharing of iTunes music files, the posting of e-birthday cards, the exchange of electronic gifts on Facebook and the writing of flattering testimonials on the Friendster community site all appear to play an important role in the nurturing process. In a post-networked society these nurturing behaviours help to create a sense of community and obligation among members of globally distributed personal networks. Indeed, these nurturing practices may help to transform a list of contacts in a 'buddy list' into what I have conceptualized as a *globally distributed fund of living knowledge*.

Challenges, choices and new media literacies

This chapter has highlighted the new opportunities that learners enjoy to exercise relationship agency and leverage the expertise of others near and far. Nevertheless, this is not the full story. This section draws attention to the associated challenges and choices students are confronted with when attempting to cultivate, nurture and activate a globally distributed fund of living knowledge and identifies some associated new media literacies.

Now social networking tools have become identified as a potentially lucrative source of business, companies have started to compete, and employ sophisticated strategies that encourage users to migrate between platforms. When I started to research students' use of social media many, but not all, used either AOL or MSN messenger on a daily basis. Later, all but one owned a Facebook account. Today, Google, Yahoo and Skype offer social services with overlapping functionality. As a result, students invariably find themselves networking, communicating and socializing with friends, colleagues and supervisors through multiple communication channels. This situation has created a somewhat fragmented communications landscape that confronts students with additional challenges and choices. For example, many students (and an increasing number of staff) who use Facebook started to talk about the breakdown between their personal and professional lives. Some felt they were being judged by how many friends they had on their Facebook buddy list, others felt they had been stalked, or openly talked about the strategies they employed to spy on romantic interests. Others complained that supervisors provided short e-mail feedback to guard their own time and avoid face-to-face supervisions. Edina felt frustrated that she could not IM (send an instant message to) her supervisor if and when required, whilst Katrina chose not to start a Facebook account to protect her privacy but later felt that students judged this kind of behaviour anti-social, if not rude and pretentious.

Even between close friends, who saw each other on a daily basis, the pro-liferation of social software could interfere with, if not damage, relationships. For example, Edina complained that she could not IM Sue Ellen because she used AOL Messenger as opposed to MSN Messenger. At the other extreme, Peter was not even aware of social software services like Friendster that were widely used by large numbers of students. This suggests that new divides are opening up, even among students who live in the same physically gated communities. The bigger picture is hard to foresee. However, it seems likely that social software might actually allow groups of students who attend established universities to safeguard their relative privileges with virtually gated communities. Nevertheless, even high-end users like Miss Lullaby, who had used social software for as long as she could remember struggled to decide which tools she should use to maintain relationships with friends and family, which of her course mates to include in her 'buddy list', or what information to make available about herself online. Today, decisions of this kind have implications personal and professional relationships and impact on a student's capacity to mobilize a personal network as a fund of living knowledge.

To elaborate, it is worth unpacking two of the central challenges required to make effective use of a globally distributed fund of living knowledge as learning resource. In particular this chapter draws attention to the challenge of: a) knowing how to know who in new mediascapes and b) resisting rela-tional agency in a space in which many of the traditional barriers are break-ing down.

Knowing how to know who in new mediascapes

Before individuals can effectively draw upon the knowledge and expertise of others, they must know who is most likely to possess the knowledge required to assist at any given time. The capacity of 'knowing how to know who' is regarded as a prerequisite for the exercise of relational agency within work-place settings (Edwards in press). With the widespread uptake of social net-working technologies it appears that this challenge becomes more complicated. Information available through personal profiles and status updates might help. For example, whilst Miss Lullaby met her medical friend 'Paul' through a social engagement, she discovered more about his work through looking at his webpage before deciding to recruit him into her inner circle of critical friends. In short, as a result of information Miss Lullaby discovered about Paul online, she identified him as a potential resource, recruited him as a virtual household member and started to nurture the relationship.

Professional websites and professional social software tools like LinkedIn that allow students to display their qualifications and prior work experience, afford students new opportunities to identify others who possess particular kinds of expertise they might later leverage. In this respect, 'knowing how to know who' in new mediascapes appears to involve a capacity to access and critically appraise personal profiles and online information to identify the skill sets of potential collaborators. Nevertheless, 'knowing how to know who' also requires students to estimate the likelihood that a potential collaborator will assist, which in turn involves a capacity to intuit their motive for doing so.

In practice, a students' capacity to intuit and align themselves in joint action on a shared object appears to depend on multiple social and historic factors. For example, Daisy could depend on the fact that all her course mates were motivated by a shared object-motive (i.e. preparing for a formal examination). In contrast, Edina and her dispersing network of former course mates shared a loosely defined shared motive (seeking employment in a specialized field) that appeared to foster an ethic of reciprocity among the group. However, other students, such as Anastasia only appeared to rely on individuals with whom they had a strong emotional bond forged in past experience.

This sensitizes one to the distinction between a social network and a fund of living knowledge. Crucially, a globally distributed fund of living knowledge involves social and emotive bonding between members who recognize themselves as a potential resource. For example, Miss Lullaby's request to the friend who 'hated' reading her work could be interpreted as a form of relational agency in a state of disrepair. However, such an interpretation underestimates the amount of nurturing work previously invested. Indeed, the sense of obligation that existed between Miss Lullaby and her friend had was embedded in a lifelong personal friendship, forged during their time together at UCLA as undergraduates and maintained during periods in which they were apart with the aid of MSN Messenger. Indeed, the bond that existed between these two former course mates appeared comparable to the bond the existed between ZeroGBoy and his mother. These observations suggest that, 'knowing how to know who' may also involve a capacity to estimate the degree to which a potential learning companion is emotionally invested in the relationship.

Resisting relational agency in new mediascapes

A capacity to resist relational agency in new mediascapes might also be considered an important form of new media literacy (Edwards and Kinti 2007).

Edina's 'skulking' strategy suggests her 'always-on' extended personal networks threatened to become a considerable source of distraction. Indeed, many students complained that they were constantly struggling to resist potential social distractions let alone requests that might involve an investment of time. The fact that requests for help, advice or assistance might be received at any time of the day or night compounded this problem. For these reasons, several of the male students deactivated or uninstalled instant messenger systems. Nevertheless, a request for assistance might be difficult to deny given that reputations, identities and friendships are often at stake. Again, this alerts us to the loss of enabling constraints provided by structured study spaces like libraries and the implicit rules (i.e. to talk quietly if at all) that protect learners from attempts by others recruit them into agendas that are not their own.

The management of dependency

Finally, the new possibilities afforded by social software to nurture and activate the distributed expertise accessible through a globally distributed fund of living knowledge remains in tension with the threat of becoming overly dependent on the expertise of others. Tools, like the track changes facility in MSWord, used extensively by Edina and Miss Lullaby, appear to facilitate the formation of intersubjective writing partnerships – guiding and focusing a collaborative writing task in a way that might facilitate the transfer of expertise between writing partners. Nevertheless, a capacity to self-regulate or (to modify the scaffolding metaphor) self-fade the level of assistance required appears important to assist progression towards autonomous performance, if indeed, autonomous performance is deemed desirable. Again Miss Lullaby's case raises some interesting questions. She claimed that her globally distributed fund of knowledge had empowered her to become less dependent on the writing centre. However, it seems that one form of dependence had simply been replaced by another. In certain respects, this appears like a natural progression from a pedagogic or androgogic mode of learning. Nevertheless, the 'always-on' learning companion is perhaps more likely to become a cognitive crutch than an assistive learning companion. Indeed, the threat of inhibited internalization is ever present in an age in which the intelligence of living breathing people can be mobilized along with the artificial intelligence of digital agents for an increasing number of tasks. Therefore, a capacity to self-fade the level of support provided and actively manage dependencies appears likely to become an important new media literacy associated with informal learning across institutional boundaries.

Summary

This chapter started by arguing that we need to look beyond electronic seminar spaces and online discussion forums established by course tutors to understand the full implications of media change for computer supported collaborative learning. It certainly lends weight to Säljö's (2004: 227) assertion that new media contributes to the creation of 'new arenas to communicate in, and new virtual contexts to develop in'. Indeed, it illustrates some of the ways that selected individuals from among a group of advanced agentive learners are appropriating the freely available 'instruments for sharing our mental abilities' that Lévy (1997: 9) had the foresight to identify as the 'most socially useful goal' for which new technologies might by appropriated. However, this assemblage of localized insider perspectives simply scratches the surface and illustrates a few of the informal learning possibilities associated with the creation, nurturing and activation of globally distributed funds of living knowledge.

At the very least, this chapter suggests that collaborative learning in online spaces purposefully established by tutors to support formal courses of study may be relatively insignificant compared to the complex hive of collaborative learning activity supported by social media that now bubbles away under the radar of the traditional university. This chapter simply opens a window onto this emergent sphere of learning activity. Further research is required to probe and fully understand these practices. The vignettes illustrate how funds of living knowledge start to form through participation in object-orientated group activities firmly situated in students' lifeworlds. However, they also illustrate students exploiting social media to build more enduring and robust globally distributed funds of knowledge that they take with them when they migrate across institutional contexts. Finally, they show how resourceful students might exercise relational agency and leverage the distributed expertise of individuals with specific knowledge and skills within their virtual 'households'. In this respect, it illustrates another highly significant genre of informal learning activity that suggests that students are now breaking away from the traditional university and advancing self-directed learning agendas that transcend institutional boundaries.

6 Learning through serious play in virtually figured worlds

Self-making is powerfully affected not only by your own interpretations of yourself, but by the interpretations others offer of your version.

(Bruner 1991: 76)

Play is also the medium of mastery, indeed of creation, of ourselves as human actors. Without the capacity to formulate other social scenes in imagination, there can be little force to a sense of self, little agency. In play we experiment with the force of our acting otherwise, of our projectivity rather than our objectivity ... Through play our fancied selves become material.

(Holland *et al.* 1998: 236)

This book has explored the various ways learners are designing and cultivating virtual environments to support personalized learning agendas. It draws attention to the ways individuals are designing cognitive ecologies, creatively appropriating web-based tools and cultivating globally distributed funds of knowledge to break away from a former dependence on life-world communities of academic practice. Further, each chapter highlights the challenges and choices confronting learners and some of the new media literacies required to exploit the full potential of the Internet as a resource for learning. However, when attempting to understand exactly what, how and why students make use of digital technologies, that is, in attempting to understand personal agency in the new media age, one is invariably forced to understand practice in relation to students' values, commitments and personal ethics which, in turn, appear related to their sense of who they are and who they might become. In short, a sociocultural approach on its own cannot account for students' individuated styles of computer use. One is also forced to understand digitally mediated practices within the personal-historic context of an individual student's life trajectory. Furthermore, when one starts to explore how advanced learners are now exploiting emerging opportunities for self-education beyond the requirements of accredited courses of study the power of identity, conceived of a powerful mediator and motivator of learning activity, becomes even more conspicuous.

In this penultimate chapter, the relationship between identity and agency comes to the foreground. The insights build on the theoretical work of four theorists: Jerome Bruner (1991); Sherry Turkle (1984, 1997); James Paul Gee (2000b, 2003, 2004); and, most importantly, Dorothy Holland *et al.* (1998). These theorists provide some deep insights into the relationship between identity and agency that can help us understand the implications of media change for learning. Their work introduces us to a way of thinking about committed self-directed learning that, I believe, can provide a deep insight into the future of (self) education.

Bruner and the narrative construction of self

In the early 1990s, under the influence of philosopher Nelson Goodman, Bruner (1991) and fellow researchers turned their attention to what they called 'self-making' and the related process of 'worldmaking'. Their thinking constitutes a more general reaction against assumptions about an 'essential self' assumed in biographical writing. In an autobiography, they argue, we 'set forth a view of what we call our "Self" and its doings, reflections, thoughts, and place in the world' (p. 67). These ruminations are not hypothetical. The research team recruited ordinary people who were given one simple instruction: 'Tell us the story of your life'. Researchers analysed the 'spontaneous', 'non-artful' autobiographies produced to explore how people constructed their life stories through narrative. The analysis showed that the process of constructing a life story could not be understood apart from the available cultural toolkit: genres, metaphors, figures of speech, and archetypes that interviewees used to construct a narrative account of their lives.

Pondering on the findings, Bruner (1991: 68) stresses, 'we have come to reject the view that a "life" is anything in itself and to believe that it is all in the constructing, of the text, or in the text-making'. From this perspective, the rules for constructing narrative, inherited from one's culture, cannot be regarded as neutral or transparent. Narrative devices inherited from the available cultural toolkit mediate our attempts to present a coherent account of our lives. Consequently the authors argue, 'like all other aspects of worldmaking, self-making (or "life-making") depends heavily upon the symbolic system in which it is conducted – its opportunities and constraints' (p. 68). From this perspective, 'Self', not unlike cognition, might be considered as distributed. Bruner summarizes these insights thus:

> It becomes plain, as one observes this process of self-formation, that it is probably a mistake to conceive of 'Self' as solo, as locked up inside one person's subjectivity, as hermetically sealed off. Rather 'Self' seems also to be inter-subjective or 'distributed' in the same way that one's 'knowledge' is distributed beyond one's head to include the friends and

colleagues to whom one has access, the notes one has filed, the books one
has on one's shelves.

(Bruner 1991, p. 76)

The version of self reflected back through interactions and dialogue appear
to play a significant role in the process of self-formation. Indeed, the authors
stress: 'what was once regarded as the most "private" aspect of our being,
turns out on closer inspection to be highly negotiable, highly sensitive to
bidding on the not so open market or one's own reference group' (p. 76).

In summary, Bruner's work sensitizes us to three issues that are helpful
for understanding identity and agency in virtually figured worlds. First,
identities are not essential; they are constructed and sustained through the
work of self-making. Second, self-making is an ongoing activity mediated by
the available cultural resources (principally genre, narrative devices and
figures of speech but also the 'books on one's shelves' and the 'notes one has
filed'). Finally, self-making is an inherently social process. Indeed, the
authors stress, 'self-making is powerfully affected not only by your own
interpretations of yourself, but by the interpretations other offer of your
version' (Bruner *et al.* 1991: 76).

These ideas provide a way of thinking about self-making as an activity
mediated by the available cultural tool kit. However, they shed little light
on the relationship between identity and agency in virtually figured worlds.
How, we might ask, does a reference group mediated by RSS feeds, Twitter
feeds and Facebook groups mediate the process of self-making?

Virtual worlds as psycho-social moratoriums for identity play

In *Life on the Screen: Identity in the Age of the Internet* (1997), Turkle explores
the new opportunities for self-making afforded by virtual role-play in text-
based Multi-User Dungeons (MUDs). Her work allows us to start thinking
about identity play in game worlds in which players take on virtual identities in practice. Data collected through virtual ethnography is used to illustrate examples of gamers exploring alternative identities that remain
repressed or inhibited in real life (or RL) through virtual role-play in the
MUD. Turkle documents instances of gender bending (men playing women
hitting on women playing men) and stories of individuals mistakenly
making a pass at an artificially intelligent flirt bot.[1] These stories might read
like amusing anecdotes. However, Turkle (1997: 185) argues that MUDs
have become 'objects-to-think-with' and reveal important insights into the
'post-modern self'.

Turkle goes on to argue that MUDs function as 'psycho-social moratoriums';
spaces that give people a certain licence to experiment with alternative lifestyles
and relationships.[2] Indeed, lamenting the demise of college countercultures she
suggests that MUDs provide a new kind of space for experimentation and self-
discovery: '[I]f our culture no longer offers an adolescent moratorium, then

virtual communities do. They offer permission to play, to try things out. This is part of what makes them attractive' (Turkle 1997: 203–204). Today online role playing games like Everquest, World of Warcraft and Second Life afford players new opportunities to create, play and experiment with alternative identities. Steinkuehler and Williams (2006) conceptualize massively multiplayer online role playing games (MMORPGs) as a 'third place' outside the restrictive structures of everyday life, which affords people the opportunity to take on alternative identities and interact with people from diverse backgrounds from all over the world. These ideas explain the growing popularity of gaming culture, not just for adolescents, but for people well into adulthood. However, in general they encourage us to understand how young people take on identities that remain repressed within real life.

Learning by being in immersive game worlds

Gee (2003) picks up and develops some of Turkle's insights in his work on the situated learning possibilities afforded by virtual role play in immersive game worlds. He argues that the identifications made through the experience of virtual role play are quite unlike those made when reading a novel or watching a movie because it is both *active* (the player actually does things) and *reflexive* (players have to make choices about how to develop their virtual personas). Further, Gee argues that the situated learning that occurs in video game play provides a model for thinking about how good learning occurs in real world situations. Interestingly this leads him to start thinking about learning as an identity-project.

> I am arguing that learning to read, or any learning for that matter, is not all about skills. It is about learning the right moves in embodied interactions in the real world or virtual worlds, moves that get one recognized as 'playing the game': that is enacting the right sort of identity for a given situation (e.g. science class in middle school).
>
> (Gee 2004: 48)

It follows that committed or intrinsically self-motivated learning occurs because the acquisition of knowledge and skills is bound-up with becoming a certain kind of person:

> People can only see a new specialist language as a gain if: (a) they recognize and understand the sorts of socially situated identities and activities that recruit the specialist language; (b) they value these identities and activities, or at least understand why they are valued; and (c) they believe they (will) have real access to these identities and activities, or at least (will) have access to meaningful (perhaps simulated) versions of them. Thus science in school is learned best and most deeply when it is, for the learner, about 'being a scientist' (of some sort) 'doing science' (of

some sort). This is why video games are so good at getting learning done. They allow people to be and do new things in new worlds, sometimes far beyond what they could be or do in the 'real' world.

(Gee 2004: 94)

Existing commercial off-the-shelf games like SimCity 2000 and Roller Coaster Tycoon position players in the role of town mayors and theme park developers. In part inspired by these games, researchers at the University of Wisconsin-Madison led by David Shaffer are now designing 'epistemic games' (2005) to give children from lower socio-economic backgrounds a 'thickly authentic' (Shaffer and Resnick 1999) experience of *being* a doctor, a lawyer, a town planner or social scientists. These games are purposefully designed to position learners in distinctive 'epistemic frames' that allow them to acquire knowledge and skills as they progress towards becoming certain kinds of virtual personas. In this respect, they might be thought of as incubators that shape learners' projective identities and help them envisage alternative social futures.

This line of research is suggestive and provocative. However, on its own, it does not capture what I think may be the most important implication of media change for self-making. To understand this process it is helpful to return to Holland *et al.*'s (1998) work on identity formation in culturally constructed or figured worlds. I believe this work can help us better understand how students are learning in virtually figured worlds that they, rather than the game designers, have designed and cultivated over the years.

Worldmaking as self-making

Holland *et al.* reject essentialist notions of self, but also reject Bruner's more individualistic notion of a self constructed in autobiography. Indeed, as discussed in Chapter 2, their work emphasizes how identities are forged through active participation in culturally constructed or figured worlds. A capacity for 'making worlds' through the activity of serious play is fundamental to the challenge of understanding human agency. The authors argue:

> The fourth context of identity is that of *making worlds*: through 'serious play', new figured worlds may come about, in the peculiarly Bakhtinian way that feeds the personal activities of particular groups, their 'signatures', into the media, the cultural genres, through which even distant others may construe their lives.
>
> (Holland *et al.* 1998: 272)

In short, through serious play people create figured worlds that manifest a version of self expressed through activity. In turn, these figured worlds mediate the activity of serious play and support learners as they acquire new skills and cultural competences as if positioned within a zone of proximal development. The authors stress:

Vygotsky's understanding of play is crucial to this argument. Just as children's play is instrumental in building their symbolic competences, upon which adult life depends, so too social play – the activities of 'free expression,' the arts and rituals created on the margins of regulated spaces and time – develops new social competencies in newly imagined communities. These new 'imaginaries' build in their rehearsal a structure of disposition, a habitus, that comes to imbue the cultural media, the means of expression, that are their legacy.

(ibid.)

I believe these ideas can help us better understand the process of self-making in virtually figured worlds. The concepts of mediation, the dialectic and the dialogic have proved useful tools for understanding why learners set about transforming the quasi-virtual contexts of their own learning and personal development throughout this book. Serious play might be conceived of as a process in which learners make worlds through playful and creative activity that afford opportunities to enact a projective identity in practice. In short, this line of thinking encourages us to understand how learners might bootstrap themselves towards the actualization of a projective identity through serious play in virtually figured worlds. Two vignettes attempt to illustrate this process. Both draw on ethnographic data in an attempt to show how advanced, resourceful and highly committed learners are designing virtual ecologies, not merely to off-load information processing tasks or leverage the knowledge and expertise of other minds, but to engage in the work of self-making.

Vignette: Clinton playing the politician in the making

Clinton geeked out on politics. He frequently attended talks by leading statesmen, engaged friends in topical debate over lunch and spent most evenings in the college bar talking to people with diverse nationalities, ethnicities and religious orientations. Access to the Internet radically expanded his capacity to engage in the world of US politics. He lived in a study room with simple furnishings and a dozen or so books on a shelf. However, when he turned on his laptop, the world of US politics came streaming into his everyday life. He read multiple online newspapers on a daily basis, programmed dozens of automatic alerts to notify him of breaking news on particular stories and he routinely watched raw video footage of important congressional debates on C-SPAN. Indeed, active participation in the figured world of politics was not a discrete activity that he 'tuned into' at particular time. Clinton metaphorically threw himself in this virtually figured world to the extent that it became integrated into his everyday life. For example, when I inquired about the degree to which these activities interfered with his studies he replied:

Umm … it takes me much longer to listen to the speeches but I can listen to the speeches when I'm getting ready to go out for the day. When I'm shaving and when I'm brushing my teeth or combing my hair I can pop up the Arnold Schwarzenegger speech or yesterday it was the John McCain speech and I can listen to Senator McCain's speech at the Republican convention (as long as I can stomach listening to his words). Now with the Democratic Convention I listen to all the speeches and everything like that…

(Clinton, MSc Social Policy)

Membership of 'Democrats Abroad' radically expanded Clinton's capacity to connect and engage with other committed Democrats from across the world wherever he might be. For example, during the case study he started to participate in an online discussion forum designed to produce a vision statement that outlined what the Democratic Party would stand for in the year 2020. Within and through this space, views, opinions and strategies were actively discussed, debated and critiqued with other young 'politicos' from around the world. Indeed, given access to a fast 'always-on' Internet connection, Clinton had transformed his humble study/bedroom into a newsroom, a communications centre and a debating chamber that positioned him at the nexus of a host of information flows and exposed him to the voices, opinions and policy agendas of political allies and adversaries from around the world.

Interestingly, when asked why it was so important to maintain this high level of immersion in the world of politics and current affairs, he replied:

Well that's who I am, I'm a policy person, I love policy, I love politics, and I love current affairs. This is what I do. Now I recognize that people don't all do that. But I enjoy it, I enjoy watching policy speeches, I enjoy listening to governmental leaders and political leaders talking about what they believe in.

(Clinton, MSc Social Policy)

Clinton now works for the Democratic Party in Washington, DC.

The vignette illustrates how a resourceful individual actively creates a virtually figured world that, in a dialectical movement, shapes his emerging sense of self. The phrase, 'that's who I am, I'm a policy person' suggests he had internalized a strong projective identity that was rehearsed and in a sense reinforced through a form of serious play. New media did not create this identity. Nevertheless, the quasi-virtual ecology that he cultivated radically expanded his capacity to enact this role. In turn this virtually figured world appeared to channel his personal development towards a strong projective identity. In this respect, the vignette illustrates one of the ways a committed learner might appropriate new media to *bootstrap themselves towards the actualization of a projective identity through a form of serious play within a virtually figured world.*

A second vignette illustrates how another student with a very different set of priorities might engage in the work of self-authoring. Here, more emphasis is placed on the ways new media enables the subject to recruit others into a virtually figured world.

Vignette: Jacob playing the environmental guy

Jacob led a principled life committed to the values of self-sufficiency, sustainable development and healthy living. In multiple respects these ethical commitments had become designed into the virtually figured world of environmental activism. Participation in multiple online groups exposed Jacob to the voices, opinions and views of environmental activists from around the world. For example, he actively participated in 'Millions against Monsanto', a web-based group dedicated to exposing the coercive marketing strategies of the food producer using genetically modified products. In addition he sourced articles on the theme of 'learnt helplessness' for a course work assignment through a Yahoo group dedicated to environmental issues. Significantly, Jacob did not simply construct himself as the 'environmental guy' in conversation. He enacted this identity on a daily basis through proactive engagement in a range of permaculture, sustainable development and environmental groups in practice.

In many respects Jacob's participation in the figured world of environmentalism defined him as a person. For example, during the course of the study he also set himself the challenge of 'hot-rodding' his own computer by assembling parts given away by the college IT officer and parts bought on eBay at discounted prices. Saving money was not the major issue. Jacob was on a mission to prove he could build a powerful computer that could play 'Half-Life 2 in all its visual glory' without 'being at the mercy of the computer manufacturers'. He encountered multiple technical problems along the way, but spent hours 'Googling' error codes and leveraging the knowledge of technical experts who responded to his posts to technical online affinity groups for hot-rodders. The machine never actually played 'Half-Life 2'. Nevertheless, this did not seem important. The activity enshrined his values and afforded him an opportunity to enact the role of the 'environmental guy' in practice. Interestingly, Jacob stressed that as a teenager he sometimes felt bullied for his unconventional beliefs and values. As a result he turned to the Internet to seek out others who shared his values. In this respect, access to a distributed community of environmentalists appeared to harden his resolve, strengthen his confidence and empower him to sustain a certain stability of self-conception.

During his year at Oxford Jacob started to actively recruit others into this virtually figured world. Initially he set up a vegetarian food co-operative that allowed college members to make bulk purchases of organic foods from an online supplier. Later he stood for election as the college environmental officer and started a campaign to extend the range of recycling services available throughout the college using an e-mail listserv called the *Grapevine* that went out to all members of the college. The tool empowered him to project a strong identity to the whole college community who, in turn, recognized and orientated to him as the 'environmental guy'.

Significantly, both Clinton and Jacob had made commitments to a particular value system that anchored emerging identities. Jacob's projective identity appeared anchored in a deep commitment to healthy living and sustainable development. Similarly, Clinton's projective identity appeared anchored by his deep commitment to public policy and left of centre politics. These ethical commitments were evident in all aspects of their practice and, in a sense, defined them as individuals. In this respect, their respective projective identities appeared to function as the *object-motives* of their lifelong learner agendas. In other words, they worked upon these identities, not unlike a gamer works at building a character in a computer game, as they engaged with participatory culture.

To abstract and generalize it is helpful to propose some new categories for understanding self-making activities in virtually figured worlds. To this end, I offer some new conceptual tools that might assist further research. This interrelated conceptual toolkit allows us to think about *virtually figured worlds* as *expanded spaces of self-authoring* that allow *committed learners* to *bootstrap themselves towards the actualization of a projective identity* through a form of *serious play* in *virtually figured worlds*. What I call *history in laptop* mediates this bootstrapping movement and allows learners to maintain a stability of self-conception across contexts. I hope these conceptual tools will prove useful for understanding how a variety of virtually figured worlds mediate learners' personal development as the Internet becomes increasingly integrated into the fabric of everyday life.

Serious play, history in laptop and committed learning

Given access and control over their virtual environments, students enjoy new opportunities to play or rehearse their projective identities in virtual worlds of their own figuration. Inspired by Vygotsky's (1978: 102) claim that 'play creates a zone of proximal development of the child', Holland *et al.* stress:

> Play is also the medium of mastery, indeed of creation, of ourselves as human actors. Without the capacity to formulate other social scenes in imagination, there can be little force to a sense of self, little agency. In play we experiment with the force of our acting otherwise, of our projectivity rather than our objectivity [...] Through play our fancied selves become material.
>
> (Holland *et al.* 1998: 236)

Indeed, new media appears to afford students new opportunities, not only to play, but also to *be* the people they wish to become. Jenkins (2006c) makes this point implicitly in his case study of Heather, the teenager who created, managed and edited *The Daily Prophet*. Likewise, Clinton and Jacob were not simply constructing a narrative account of their lives in retrospect, they were enacting their projective identities on a daily basis through serious play within their virtually figured worlds. Indeed, over time their 'fancied selves' became material through serious play in virtually figured worlds generated by their own purposive activities.

Development through serious play is certainly not a new mode of personal development. However, what appears distinctive is the range and complexity of props and scaffolds available to support role-playing activities. Vygotsky draws attention to the fact that play can be stimulated with simple props that stimulate imaginary play. Indeed, drama teachers invariably stimulate dramatic improvisation with a box full of simple props: masks or everyday objects – a briefcase and bowler hat, or sword and a pirate's hat for example – that respectively suggest the figured worlds of city finance and piracy on the high seas. These props thereby help the drama student construct a figured world in their imagination. In a sense the figured world signified by the props mediates the activity of improvisational drama as the actors play out their roles within the imaginary context created.

The vignettes presented suggest that access to digital tools and resources radically extend the available props or stimuli that individuals might appropriate as they learn through serious play. Indeed, Clinton and Jacob were not simply experimenting with alternative identities that remained repressed in real life. They were actively seeking opportunities to enact their projective identity through a form of serious play in quasi-virtual contexts of their own figuration. In this respect these virtually figured worlds allowed both students to take on professional roles and responsibilities and *be* the people they aimed to become.

Significantly, Clinton and Jacob were proud of their personal histories; personal histories that had become enshrined in their virtually figured worlds and continued to mediate their sense of self and community as they crossed contexts. The concept *history in laptop* helps us understand this fundamentally new form of mediation.

History in laptop

In an age in which an increasing number of students' connection with former selves appears to be mediated through the laptop computers they carry around with them in their backpacks, it appears we need new conceptual tools to understand how and why past experiences might continue to mediate students' actions and behaviour. The category *history in laptop* serves this purpose. If *history in person* is conceptualized as internalized identity in practice stored as patterns of neuron firings in a biological brain, *history in laptop* might be conceptualized as identity in digitally mediated practice that has become externalized and recorded as patterns of computer code and symbolic representations in a learner's virtually figured world. Not unlike *history in person*, *history in laptop* has a certain 'agenda and momentum of its own'; it sustains a subject in a particular identity, such as the 'policy person' or the 'environmental guy', over time. Nevertheless, there are some important distinctions.

Significantly, *history in laptop* does not depend on the human memory. It may be lost as a result of a hard drive failure or accidental deletion of data. Further, *history in laptop* is non-material. It resides in each individual's virtually figured world rather than a physical computer. Indeed, it can quite literally be transferred across physical-state devices when, for example, a student transfers documents and settings to a new computer. Increasingly *history in laptop* resides in online spaces, such as the 'Democrats Abroad' affinity space and social software profiles like Facebook. Consequently, *history in laptop* is more robust than *history in person*. Students can take it with them as they move across institutional contexts. In multiple respects, *history in laptop* works to keep the past present, it reminds learners who they are, and reminds them what they are supposed to be doing when they sit down at their computers.

Committed learning

Committed learning describes a mode of learning in which the learning activity is helping the learner to work on their projective identity. In a sense, learning becomes committed when the learning is in alignment with an individual's projective identity. In contrast learners who are forced to engage in activities that are out of alignment with their projective identities are likely to become disinterested or distracted. Clinton and Jacob were both committed learners. They passionately engaged in the activity of learning about democratic politics and environmentalism because these activities were helping them work on their projective identities. They received no formal accreditation or external reward for these extra-curricular activities. Nevertheless, they were deeply invested in becoming certain kinds of persons and their commitments to these projective identities provided a powerful motivator for these self-directed learning activities.

In Chapter 4 Anastasia's dedication to teaching herself statistics only makes sense when we understand this in relation to her commitment to putting social work on a more scientific footing. In this case the learning activity was in alignment with her projective identity. Similarly, the time Edina invested in nurturing a globally distributed network of contacts within the NGO sector cannot be fully understood without understanding her deep commitment to fighting the injustices afflicting refugees around the world. In this respect, the notion of committed learning draws our attention to the need to understand learners' identities as powerful mediators and motivators of learning activity.

Virtually figured worlds as expanded spaces of self-authoring

For Holland *et al.*'s spaces that allow individuals to engage in the work of self-making in collaboration with others are conceptualized as a *space of authoring*. They write:

The world must be answered – authorship is not a choice – but the form of the answer is not predetermined [. . .] authoring is a matter of orchestration: of arranging the identifiable social discourses/ practices that are one's resources in a time and space defined by others' standpoints in activity, that is, in a social field conceived as the ground of responsiveness.

(Holland *et al*. 1998: 272)

In their case of disenfranchised peoples living in developing countries, the variety of cultural resources they might draw upon to resist appears extremely limited. For example, Holland *et al*. (1998: 3–18) describe a lower caste Indian woman who cannot bring herself to enter the house of a higher caste neighbour despite the fact she has been invited into the house by researchers. She improvises a solution and, rather spectacularly, climbs up the side of a house to get up on to a balcony rather than violate the dictates of the figured worlds of caste. Her action constitutes a creative improvisation in a particular situation that enables her to negotiate an immaterial yet forceful internalized constraint. The authors stress:

Human agency comes through this art of improvisation; the space of authoring includes Vygotsky's zone of proximal development. The 'voices' that make up Vygotsky's space of authoring are to an 'author' as Vygotsky's instructing adults are to the neophyte: they do not so much compel rote action as extend, through their support, the competences, the 'answerability,' of persons to operate in such as diverse yet powerful social universes.

(Holland *et al*. 1998: 272)

Nevertheless, the improvisation enables the lower caste Indian women to conform rather than reject her position within the figured worlds of caste. She has no prior experience of living in a society where the rules and prohibitions of the caste system do not apply.

As today's students move through higher education they invariably move across contexts engaging in relationships with others from diverse cultural backgrounds. Consequently, individuals have access to a wider repertoire of 'voices' to draw upon as cultural resources when compelled to 'make an answer'. They might also draw upon fictional voices they have experienced through the media of literature, film, drama or television. This line of reasoning suggests that the polyphony of voices that constitute the dialogic imagination in advanced contemporary society 'extend, through their support, the competences, the "answerability," of persons to operate in such as diverse yet powerful social universes' (Holland *et al*. 1998: 272). However, if the hybrid multicultural context of complex modern societies expands the space of authoring, it seems feasible that access to a hybrid, global participatory culture expands it further still.

In an emergent web-based participatory culture learners have choices. Further, as illustrated throughout this book, given the proliferation of information flows, special interest groups and communication channels, today's students often find themselves confronted with an anxiety of choice. In many respects, this places additional burdens of responsibility. Nevertheless, it also affords new opportunities. The designability of new media allows individuals to take more of the onus of responsibility for identifying, orchestrating, and regulating their exposure to various voices within a virtually figured world and shut out undesirable voices as they engage in the work of self-authoring.

Lifelong learning beyond institutional boundaries

If one embraces this way of thinking about identity, agency and personal development it becomes interesting to consider: a) how projective identities are formed and take shape in early childhood; b) how virtually figured worlds might empower individuals to resist the overbearing pressure to conform; and c) to understand how virtually figured worlds function as spaces of self-authoring that transcend institutional contexts. A final extended vignette attempts to illustrate how new media empowers a student to take more control over his lifelong learning agenda. It works at an ontogenetic level of analysis.

Vignette: Jim playing the 'human rights guy'

Jim invested considerable time engaging in the virtually figured worlds of human rights activism. He actively participated in the Economic and Social Rights Network, Business and Human Rights, Human Rights and The Shelter Network as well as subscribing to alert services to track specific news stories. For example, he became very concerned about the issue of forced evictions in Zimbabwe and programmed a Google alert bot to automatically e-mail himself any relevant news articles.

Jim's level of participation in these online groups fluctuated over time and often depended on circumstance. For example, he argued that his engagement with COHRE (Centre on Housing Rights and Evictions) often resulted in him receiving four to five e-mails a day. The work was sporadic and Jim simply lurked and monitored the development of many of the issues. However, occasionally something 'came up' in which he became heavily involved. Such was the issue regarding forced evictions in Zimbabwe. He commented that he 'really pushed the envelope out on that one'. Indeed, despite the investment of time, Jim was highly committed to these extra-curricular activities even though they often interfered with his studies. Asked why he spent so much time participating in multiple online human rights groups he replied:

Because I think this is the way it should be. And I think there should be solidarity between these different activities and one thing I can bring to it is – I've read a lot in that field and I'm abreast of a lot of developments so I can be of assistance by providing information.

(Jim, MSt Law)

In short, Jim had internalized a deep commitment to a particular set of values that was now shaping his digitally mediated practices which in turn shaped his emerging sense of self.

This account suggests how Jim's virtually figured world empowers him to learn through a form of serious play. However, it does not explain his steadfast commitment to these time consuming extra-curricular activities. To understand this we need to adopt a historical stance and understand the evolution of Jim's projective identity from his early school years. The following section shows Jim appropriating multiple cultural tools to forge a strong projective identity. In turn, it shows how Jim's virtually figured world started to function as a space of self-authoring that empowered him to enact this identity in practice. Finally, it shows how he then used *history in laptop* to resist the overbearing influence of a lifeworld that threatened this identity and escape a double bind.

Jim was not particular remarkable at school; he described himself as an able student but not particularly distinguished. Indeed, he described school as a 'mixed experience'. However, he described his father as an 'encyclopaedia of knowledge' who had a 'massive study' with 'thousands of books' and who had a 'massive influence on his intellectual development'. Further, he explained how he became deeply interested in politics and justice-related issues through his relationship with his father. Indeed, he recalled spending hours talking about politics, economics, racism and his favourite topic, 'What's wrong with capitalism?' As a result, he argued that from 'at least the age of eleven' he had a strong sense that he would become a doctor or some kind of job that involved 'helping others'.

Upon leaving school, Jim gained a place to study philosophy at Ottawa University. Two books that he read played a highly significant role in shaping Jim's projective identity. The first was the *International Charter of Human Rights*, the second was a reading of selected works by Friedrich Nietzsche. He argued that the *International Charter of Human Rights* provided him with a focus and a new way to think about 'justice-related issues' without committing himself to his father's radical left-wing political views. In the philosophy of Nietzsche, he found the concept of 'self-overcoming' compelling. Indeed, Jim said that these works encouraged him 'to really consciously think about what kind of person I was and how I could make myself better'. As a result, he set about trying to 'improve himself in many different ways in many different directions'. To this end, he started reading the classic literary texts, started conducting independent reading of 'scientific journals' and starting learning the Japanese martial art of ju-jitsu.

After graduating, Jim travelled. He planned to study the poor and oppressed in Ecuador, he planned to 'try and work out what their problems were' by conducting a person-to-person study and then dedicating the rest of his life to solving them. However, this study quickly developed into a form of activism. He soon found himself providing fellow human rights activists with English tuition free of charge. He had recognized the importance of the English language as a way to help these activists promote their causes. Further, he set about securing financial support for the project and established the school as an NGO with charitable status. It was also at this time he first started to use computers in a proactive way. He needed to 'put together parcels' that included 'timetables, charts and a few graphics' to make promotional material using MS Publisher; activities that combined his internalized ethic of 'self-overcoming' with a desire to promote 'human rights'.

After some time living in Ecuador and building up the NGO, he decided that his ability to tackle issues of poverty and injustice as a teacher of English were somewhat limited. Consequently he resolved to return to Canada and study the legalities of international human rights at McGill University. Jim recalled that there 'was no single group at McGill dedicated to international human rights' so he decided to set one up. This involved the extensive use of e-mail to co-ordinate the group's activities. Not unlike the NGO project, the group soon attracted like minded people and grew into a series of seminars and workshops with visiting speakers from far and wide. As a result he became well known among members of the faculty with whom he often found himself participating in informal discussions about legal and development issues.

Upon graduation, Jim found himself in considerable debt and took a job at a corporate law firm in New York. He described the year at the law firm as, 'the worst year of my life in many ways'. When asked to explain, Jim replied, 'Well, I went from being the human rights guy at McGill to a corporate lawyer in New York. Those were at the polar opposites of the spectrum ... So for me it was extremely difficult'. The conflict between his identity as a corporate lawyer and human rights campaigner appeared to be a source of considerable stress. The role he stepped into did not feel authentic. Further, he was constantly required to reinvent his former identity in order to fit in with the prevailing ethos of the corporate law firm. Further, given the long working hours the job demanded, he had little time to engage in human rights activities outside of those working hours. Nevertheless, he remained active as an online participant in various online human rights groups throughout this period. Then, having saved money and paid off his debts, Jim applied and was accepted to study for a MSt in law at Oxford where he able to fully reconnect with the world of human rights activism through virtually figured worlds that kept him connected to former versions of self – the human rights activist in Ecuador.

From the personal-historic perspective, the subject's continued participation in the figured world of human rights activism, at first perplexing, starts to make perfect sense. Indeed, engagement with this virtually figured world no longer appears like an additional activity. Rather, it appears essential for understanding commitment and success. Jim felt alienated and inauthentic whilst working as a corporate lawyer. Learning about corporate law was not a committed activity. Nevertheless, his laptop afforded access to another sphere of activity and a former practiced identity – the NGO worker in Ecuador – which gave a sense of meaning and purpose to his life. He did not receive any kind of financial reward for these activities. Nevertheless, these activities, mediated by *history in laptop*, were in alignment with a projective identity forged through the conversations with his father and enacted as an NGO worker in Ecuador and functioned as the objective-motive of his life-long learning agenda. The move to Oxford helped him get out of the rut and into a groove that allowed him to progress rapidly towards the actualization of a projective identity. Indeed, when studying law at Oxford, Jim appeared actively engaged in the process of identity reconstruction.

In order to participate in multiple online groups, Jim maintained six e-mail accounts. He used these strategically, not only to organize his mail, but as tool to project different versions of self to different communities. An extended extract of dialogue recorded in response to the question, 'Why do you need six e-mail addresses?' suggests the complexity of the identity play involved.

JIM: I have my Oxford account, I have my McGill alumni account that I use all the time, I have my CISDL (Centre for International Sustainable Development Law) account because I'm a research fellow there, and I have my COHRE account, and then I have my Hotmail account that I kept just because I'd given that to a lot of people over the years and I have a Mac.com account which I never use, it was something that was given to me.

RF: So why do you need all these e-mail accounts?

JIM: I have four of my accounts downloaded to my laptop every day, and I typically send from each account often. And I use them as ways to categorize my work too. So I don't want someone whom I am working with at CISDL to send mail to my Oxford account – which happens often and I have to tell people to send to my CISDL account because I want to keep all those messages in the same folder.

RF: So it helps you compartmentalize your life and you play a different role, in these different communities and you want to keep those roles separate?

JIM: That's right. And of course I exploit the different identities. Well, if I'm contacting someone who is going to respect an Oxford account more then I allow it, but if I want to come across as someone who is possibly more established then a DPhil candidate I might want to come across as a research fellow, in which case I use CISDL and then sign it with my signature at the bottom.

> RF: Why would that give you a more professional status?
>
> JIM: Say I'm dealing with a senior partner at a law firm for instance on a topic that I deal with at the CISDL. I'm going to use that address so that it doesn't betray the fact that I'm also a student which is exactly what happened in one case. Or if I'm liaising with some activists I might want to write from my COHRE account or if I might have to deal with a government official and I want them to send to my Oxford account because that carries more weight with the person who is on the other end of it ... depending on who it is.
>
> RF: So you're very aware of the identity that your e-mail address conveys and the credibility that it's going to give you and you're conscious of constructing the right identity for the right person?
>
> JIM: That's right.
>
> RF: That's fascinating.

Jim was acutely aware of the implicit messages the e-mail address conveyed to people with whom he corresponded. Moreover, he tactically exploited these multiple online identities (Jim the Oxbridge law student, Jim the NGO worker, Jim the COHRE consultant) to maximize his credibility. In short, Jim strategically shifted between identities and registers to suit his changing purposes as he enacted multiple roles within a virtually figured world of his own figuration. Even whilst working from the comfort of his student flat, or from his favourite spot in the back of the law library down the road, Jim was at once a postgraduate student, an NGO worker, a human rights activist, a barrister in training, a respected fellow of the International Centre for Sustainable Development and a paid consultant for COHRE. He was at once the recipient of information, the disseminator of information, an apprentice and a tutor, a legitimate peripheral participant and a pro-active mobilizer, an advisor, and activist, a facilitator and a researcher. Indeed, the identity he acquired through this diverse range of activities served as a foundation and a source of energy that was propelling him forwards towards his projective identity.

Summary

This chapter illustrates that resourceful students are bootstrapping themselves towards the actualization of a projective identity through serious play in virtually figured worlds. In other words, these advanced agentive students appeared to have assumed full responsibility for their own personal development and actively constructed virtually figured worlds that mediated the process of self-formation and empowered them to literally *be* the people they aimed to become. The opportunities virtually figured worlds afford for self-making activity beyond particular lifeworld communities of practice embedded in institutional contexts seem highly significant. For the first time in history new media ecologies afford individuals opportunities to escape the overbearing influence of identities forged in a particular lifeworld communities and take more control over their own personal development as they shape their sense of self and community from the outside. Indeed, this chapter suggests that we have entered a new era in the history of human agency. For these reasons it appears important to better understand this emergent mode of self-directed lifelong learning. It is hoped that the concepts offered might facilitate this process.

7 The decentring of the traditional university

Introduction

This book set out to explore the implications of media change for the future of (self) education in an age in which an emergent web-based participatory culture is displacing a top-down culture industry model of education that has evolved around the medium of the book. The emergent genres of learning activity, identified in Chapters 3 through 6 can help us understand this process of cultural transition. Each chapter illustrates some of the ways advanced resourceful students are now breaking away from traditional modes of learning and instruction. Moreover, each chapter offers conceptual tools and typologies that can help us understand how a new generation of students are designing radically personalized cognitive ecologies, creatively appropriating digital tools as learning resources and advancing self-directed learning agendas in quasi-virtual contexts of their own figuration. Overall, this movement suggests that as a result of media change we have witnessed *a shift in the locus of agency for regulating and managing learning* that may be resulting in the decentring of the traditional university.

The vignettes and examples offered help to ground and anchor the work of conceptual development. Nevertheless, there is a danger that, to use a metaphor, the reader might fail to see the wood for the trees. In this final chapter an attempt is made to zoom out and provide a model for conceptualizing this period of cultural transition at a wider systemic level. The aim is to tease out the implications and indicate some new directions for research and development that could support student learning in participatory cultures that transcend institutional boundaries.

Two approaches to understanding the implications of media change

The full implications of media change may only become visible with the benefit of hindsight. As Marshal McLuhan (1994: 8) once argued with respect to the impact of the invention of the light bulb on Western civilization, ubiquitous Internet access has started to impact upon our lives in profound but sometimes subtle and invisible ways. Further, as insiders caught up in a process of cultural transition it is not always possible to see the most profound and significant ways media change is reshaping every aspect of everyday life. This poses considerable challenges for those wishing to generalize and forecast the mid- and long-term implications. Therefore, it is worth reflecting on two different strategies media theorists have used in an attempt to tease out the wider implications.

The first strategy involves making an imaginary leap into the future. The opening lines of Castells' *The Rise of the Networked Society* are telling in this respect:

> Towards the end of the second millennium of the Christian era several events of historical significance transformed the social landscape of human life. A technological revolution, centred around information technologies, began to reshape, at accelerated pace, the material basis of society.
>
> (Castells 2000 vol. 1: 1)

In these somewhat dramatic opening lines Castells adopts of the voice of a historian of the future reflecting back upon the current period of transition in an attempt to identify the most significant trends. In the book he proceeds to develop an analogy between the Industrial Revolution of the nineteenth century and the Information Technology Revolution of the later twentieth century. The results are illuminating. Nevertheless, this strategy risks mapping the old onto the new and leading one to conclusions that fail to take account of some of the more mundane media change that is experienced in everyday life.

Throughout this book, rather than making speculative leaps of the imagination, I have attempted to develop models for understanding the implications of media change through the concrete analysis of students' digital mediated practices. The insights gained are presented in the vignettes that provide various localized insider perspectives on this process of cultural transition. This strategy takes inspiration from the deep insights gained from small scale ethnographic studies that explore young people's engagement with participatory cultures (Jenkins 2006a; Tobin 1998). Such an approach reduces the risk of making grand generalizations that fail to grasp how media change is experienced in everyday life. It constitutes a viable alternative to the leap into the future strategy used by Castells. However, at times it is too easy to get lost in the details. Jenkins discusses this problem in a passage in which he reflects on the process of writing Convergence Culture:

> Writing this book has been challenging because everything seems to be changing at once and there is no vantage point that takes me above the fray. Rather than trying to write from an objective vantage point, I

describe in this book what this process looks like from various localised perspectives – advertising executives struggling to reach a changing market, creative artists discovering new ways to tell stories, educators tapping informal learning communities, activists deploying new resources to shape a political future, religious groups contesting the quality of their cultural environs, and of course, various fan communities who are early adopters and creative users of emerging media.

(Jenkins 2006a: 12)

This book adopts a similar strategy in an attempt to get 'above the fray' and tease out the implications of media change for higher education. It is also hoped that the vignettes presented throughout provide a patchwork of localized insider perspectives that can help us make some legitimate claims about future of (self) education more generally. In what follows the reader is presented with some models and conceptual tools that might facilitate this process.

Conceptualizing higher education with the aid of Engeström's extended mediational trianglev

In order to reconceptualize the journey through higher education as an identity-project directed towards the actualization of a projective identity it is helpful to use a modified version of Engeström's (1987, 1999) extended mediation triangle. This model may also help to illuminate the interconnected nature of many of the tensions and contradictions that emerge in this book and help us understand the implications of media change at a wider systemic level. The model is grounded in a study of graduate students living and learning in the context of a networked university. However, given that this group are early adopters of new technologies and innovators of new practices, in time it may also serve to conceptualize the predicament of learners in a changing media environment more generally. Of course, further research would be required to establish whether or not this is indeed the case. Thus, the following should be considered as a working hypothesis designed to provoke debate.

The diagram attempts to conceive of the university as an activity system in the process of transformation as a new generation of digital tools and resources become accessible through fast 'alway-on' Internet connectivity. It adapts a theoretical schema devised by Engeström (1987, 1999) to conceptualize object-orientated activities mediated by multiple cultural tools. Significantly, Vygotsky's subject-tool-object triangle (top) used to conceptualize tool-mediated action is extended with the additional of three categories: rules (or constraints); community; and division of labour (bottom row).

Postgraduate students are conceived of as the subjects of the activity system. A narrow view might assume that they attend university to gain formal academic qualifications. However, such a perspective ignores a variety

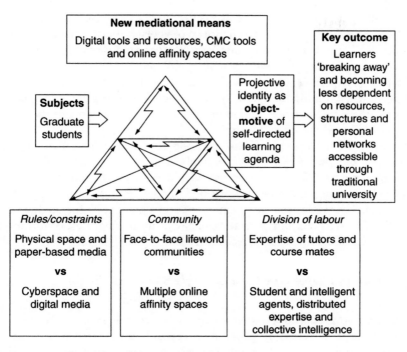

Figure 7.1 Higher education as self-making activity.

of practices related to informal and recreational activities in which students learn and develop. Consequently, this model assumes that students go to university for a variety of reasons: to gain academic qualifications; to build personal networks; to find space and time for self-education; to gain valuable experiences through participation in clubs and societies; to make friends, find partners, and prepare themselves for the jump into the job market. Students' identities are formed and take shape as they engage in these activities. Consequently, all of these activities might be subsumed under the umbrella term of self-making activities.

In the diagram, students' projective identities (right) are conceived as the personal object-motives of a lifelong learning agenda that includes both formal (accredited) and informal (self-directed) learning activities. Students work on these identities as they progress through higher education. This enables us to understand self-making activities as part of a lifelong learning agenda directed towards the actualization of a projective identity. Such a move risks subverting a central tenet of Leont'ev's (1979) version of activity theory. For Leont'ev, activity systems (such as the primeval hunt) are defined by and directed towards a shared object (such as the killing of deer) that satisfies the needs of the whole community. From this perspective, the idea that an individual's *projective identity* might serve as the object-motive of a lifelong learning agenda might appear too individualistic. Nevertheless, following Bruner (1991: 76), here self-making activity is conceived as a collective activity that is 'powerfully affected not only by your own interpretations of yourself, but by the interpretations others offer of your version'. Similarly, the notion of *bootstrapping oneself towards that actualization of a projective identity through serious play in a virtually figured world* (Chapter 6) is conceived of as a distributed process of self-formation in which information flows, participation in online groups and connections to others are extremely important. Thus, self-making remains the end point of a distributed and collective activity.

The bottom of the triangle draws attention to the *rules* (or constraints), the *community* and the *division of labour* involved in learning conceived of as self-making activity. The zig-zag arrows within the triangle and the versus sign in the boxes suggest the tensions created as a set of once-dominant practices is displaced or subverted by an emergent set of practices associated with new media. The tensions and contradictions relating to the rules, community and division of labour are now discussed in turn.

Physical space and paper-based media vs cyberspace and digital media

The *rules* or *constraints* box directs our attention to the tensions between learning activities mediated by physical spaces and paper-based media (i.e. the traditional university) to learning activities mediated by cyberspace and digital media (i.e. the networked university). Internet access clearly offers students new opportunities. Nevertheless, the use of digital tools and resources also confronts individuals with new challenges and choices. This book draws attention to both the new opportunities and the new challenges and choices confronting students as they attempt to negotiate the fault lines of media convergence. Following Wertsch *et al.* (1995), interpretations that emphasize the new opportunities are regarded as 'the cup half full perspective', whilst interpretations that emphasize the challenges and choices confronting learners are regarded as the 'cup half empty perspective'.

The cup half full interpretation tends to celebrate the new opportunities for students to learn independently, at their own pace, leveraging digital tools and online resources to address authentic learning needs if and when required. This perspective might be caricatured as the uncritical utopianism fuelling the 'personalization' discourse (Green *et al.* 2005). In contrast, the 'cup half empty' interpretation foregrounds the enabling constraints designed into physical learning spaces (libraries, seminar rooms and private study areas) that have evolved over centuries to protect learners from disorientation, information overload and the perennial threat of distraction (Crook 2002; Crook and Light 2007). Many of these enabling constraints are lost when students start to turn to the Internet as their primary learning resource. Indeed, writers, editors and publishers invest a great deal of time reflecting on the design and layout of paper-based learning media (e.g. textbooks, reference manuals and encyclopaedias) that serve to scaffold, structure and guide the learner as they use these resources to study. Their intelligence becomes designed into paper-based learning media. Similarly, educators invest a great deal of time selecting suitable materials and designing and structuring learning activities that scaffold student learning. When learning online much of this structure is lost. As a result, students must start to take on more of the onus of responsibility for selecting and evaluating materials and establishing structures that scaffold their own learning activity. I conceptualize this cultural shift in terms of a *shift in the locus of agency for managing and regulating learning*.

Face-to-face lifeworld communities vs multiple online special interest groups

Access to social media and participatory media empowers students to break away from a dependence on tutors and course mates and cultivate distributed learning networks that transcend institutional boundaries. However, this does not negate the continued importance of lifeworld communities of academic practice. The *community* box in Figure 7.1 directs our attention to the tensions confronting learners as they attempt to access, manage and negotiate the knowledge and expertise of other people both on- and offline. The cup half full interpretation draws attention to the opportunities learners now enjoy to leverage the distributed expertise of others through *globally distributed funds of living knowledge* and learn through participation in a variety of online special interest groups. In contrast, the 'cup half empty' interpretation draws attention to the additional burdens of responsibility placed upon students who attempt to take advantage of these new opportunities afforded. In particular, Chapter 5 identifies the challenge of nurturing distributed funds of living knowledge and the difficulty of *knowing how to know who* might be capable and willing to assist. Furthermore, when learning through participation in online special interest groups, students must remain on guard against the dangers of addictive and time-wasting modes of participation. Resourceful students identify the dominant agendas at work within online spaces, avoid dependency relationships and resist the strategies employed by commercial agendas struggling to recruit their attention. Moreover, advanced learners remain mindful of the various ways participation in online culture mediated their priorities, values and sense of community.

Shifts in the division of labour required to engage in advanced knowledge work

The third box (bottom right in Figure 7.1) draws our attention to the shifting distributions of cognitive labour required to engage in advanced knowledge work. From a sociocultural perspective, the cognitive load required to complete a task is distributed between the biological brain and the cognitive tools used to work on specific tasks. With the widespread adoption and use of computers many routine cognitive chores (i.e. literature searching, filtering, proofing) were delegated to quasi-intelligent agents. Moreover, the cognitive load required to complete assignments and dissertations is invariably shared between course mates and tutors. Access to networked computers is associated with additional shifts in the division of cognitive labour. Indeed, this book illustrates that advanced knowledge work often involves remote learning companions and the distributed expertise available in online special interest groups. In these cases the cognitive load is shared or distributed between two or more people working together on a shared object. This can lead to efficiency gains. Nevertheless, individual students must take on more of the onus of responsibility for managing and regulating how, with what, and with whom the cognitive labour for advanced knowledge work is distributed.

The 'cup half full' interpretation draws attention to the way students, like Timothy, use dedicated applications (like the MRI-Cro brain image tool) to engage in advanced knowledge work and leverage the expertise of others if and when required. In contrast, the 'cup half empty' interpretation highlights the dangers of *inhibited internalization* and threat of dependency on particular tools, resources and remote learning companions. However, overall this box highlights that learning in what Perkins (1997) described as 'person solo' mode is no longer an option. A student's capacity to engage in advanced knowledge work depends on the information processing powers of 'person plus', a range of digital tools, resources and remote learning companions in additional to locally available resources.

Are we witnessing the decentring of the traditional university?

The 'outcomes' box highlights what this book identifies as the key implication of media change for the learning. It suggests that students who break away from traditional lifeworld communities of learners and start cultivating globally distributed funds of living knowledge are becoming less dependent on paper-based learning media and lifeworld communities of academic practice. In this respect, students are no longer dependent on the resources and communities supported by the traditional university to the same degree. For these reasons, I suggest that as a result of media change we are witnessing the *decentring of the traditional university* in the everyday lives of university students.

The decentring metaphor appears appropriate. It does not negate the continued importance of paper-based resources, structured learning environments, or activities orchestrated by tutors and lecturers. The decentring metaphor simply draws attention to fact that students are no longer dependent on tools, resources and structured courses of study to the same degree. Indeed, in contexts in which Internet access has become near-ubiquitous this process of decentring is somewhat inevitable. For example, in a world in which, as Timothy found, it is quicker to look up a word in the *Oxford English Dictionary Online* than the *Oxford English Dictionary* sitting on one's bookshelf, changes in routine, everyday practices should be expected. Critically, this book has stressed that media change is driven from the bottom up as students creatively appropriate new media forms, as they become available, to address authentic learning needs. In this respect, the process of decentring is and always has been driven by innovations at the microgenetic level.

One cannot really fully appreciate this process of cultural transition by remaining at the sociocultural level of analysis. In Chapters 5 and 6 it became apparent that we need to adopt a personal-historic perspective in order to understand how and why students appropriate new media forms to serve their changing purposes over time. The same logic applies when it comes to understanding the process of decentring at a wider systemic level. Historically educators have appropriated new meditational means from slide rules to pocket calculators, as they become available, to expand learning opportunities and address authentic learning needs. As a result, the centrality of traditional learning media (i.e. textbooks) and traditional modes of knowledge dissemination (i.e. photocopied handouts) are displaced by practices that exploit the affordances of new media (i.e. interactive web-based tutorials and institutional virtual learning environments). This suggests that the process of decentring is an ongoing process that will continue to evolve as new technologies become available and displace the old. Nevertheless, this process of decentring may have become more visible in recent years due to the rapidity of media change. Indeed, within the time span it took to research and write this book students all around the world have witnessed fundamental displacements in their relative dependence on traditional paper-based versus digital media as a learning resource. In turn, hybrid ecologies that combine the old and the new are commonplace. For example, we now find students using multiple web-based statistics tutorials in combination with a traditional textbook to teaching themselves multivariate analysis. This brings about reconfigurations in the relative utility of each resource with overlapping functionality.

As the new media becomes layered on top of the old further displacements should be expected. In turn, we should expect resourceful students, like Wertsch's (1998: 23–72) pole vaulters, to seek out and exploit the new possibilities to gain an edge in an increasingly competitive academy. Thus, in the vignettes we glimpse a new and emergent culture of learning in which individuals are turning to the Internet as the primary site of knowledge, creatively appropriating web-based statistics tutorials, using Wikipedia to prepare themselves for entrance into the British legal establishment, and nurturing personal relationships with potential learning companions through the posting of away messages on MSN Messenger. More recently I have interviewed students who have shared vodcasts of TED (Technology

Entertainment and Design) talks on Facebook, use LiveLeak.com to develop their interest in 'just war theory' and used YouTube to research the evolving relationship between break-dance and hip hop music.

This book has also emphasized that it is not possible to understand how these displacements are experienced, nor how new media forms are appropriated by remaining focused on the technology. For example, it was not possible to understand how Ardash started to use the Amazon.com book recommendation system to gain an insight into the various 'webs of influence' between authors without understanding his internalized commitment to read widely and broaden his mind during his time at Oxford. Similarly, in order to understand how Jim used Wikipedia to prepare himself for entrance into the British legal establishment it was necessary to understand his personal history, his values and his commitment to a strong projective identity. In each case we witness students taking control, breaking away and buying into the ethic of a globalized participatory culture; a culture that comes into being through a commitment to a certain set of values, priorities and possible future selves as much as access to a particular set of digital tools.

This model of cultural and systemic change is compatible with Jenkins' (2006a) *Convergence Culture* model that draws attention to the way disruptive technologies like Napster and the distributed file-sharing communities it supported, subverted and undermined the monolithic control of the music industry, or the way Skype Internet telephony has started to unsettle the power, control and financial interests invested in the telecommunications industry. It is also compatible with a far older discourse, inspired by the dialectical materialism of Marx and Engels (1970) that argues that real and sustained systemic transitions are always driven by invisible breakthroughs from below as thousands of individuals, working through existing contradictions, innovate new practices that eventually bring about systemic change. Indeed, Ilyenkov, the philosopher of dialectical materialism whom Vygotsky and his followers adopted as their philosophical mentor, argued that sustained systemic changes cannot happen in any other way:

> In reality it always happens that a phenomenon which later becomes universal originally emerges as an individual, particular, specific phenomenon, as an exception from the rule. It cannot actually emerge in any other way. Otherwise history would have a rather mysterious form. Thus, any new improvement of labour, every new mode of man's action in production, before becoming generally accepted and recognised, first emerges as a certain deviation from previously accepted and codified norms. Having emerged as an individual exception from the rule in the labour of one or several men, the new form is then taken over by others, becoming in time a new universal norm. If the new norm did not originally appear in this exact manner, it would never become a really universal form, but would exist merely in fantasy, in wishful thinking.
>
> (Ilyenkov 1982: 83–84, cited in Engeström 2005: 214)

If this model of cultural or systemic change is accurate, then it is plausible that the practices of advanced, agentive learners who are emerging as the exception from the rule may, in time, be taken over by others and become a new universal norm. Indeed, if this model is accurate, then it seems more than likely that the documented practices of the postgraduate students studied and the tentative hypotheses proposed do indeed provide a glimpse into the future of higher education in particular and, given time, the future of (self) education more generally. Obviously, further work will be required to ascertain exactly how this process of cultural change continues. This is particularly important now that many so-called Web 2.0 technologies have come to maturity and tools such as Wikipedia, YouTube, Facebook and social bookmarking technologies have become integrated into the routine practice of learners in homes, schools and universities around the world.

Implications for educational policy and practice

The implications for educational policy are profound and wide-ranging. Significantly, this model implies that change does not come about as a result of the decisions taken by centralized committees and university administrators. In a sense centralized services are in the business of playing catch up. As students seize control of the means of knowledge production and dissemination, it seems that they are already making choices that policymakers and those in positions of authority will be compelled to take heed of. Failure to do so would risk leaving the educational provisions provided by the traditional university somewhat obsolete. In many respects, it shifts attention away from thinking about how centralized services might best support student learning towards thinking about how we might empower all students to become more resourceful, independent lifelong learners capable of exploiting the full potential of the Internet as a resource for (self) education.

Indeed, over the first decade of the twenty-first century successive waves of studies have highlighted the widening gap between learning in and out of formal educational contexts and started to foreground the importance of empowering learners to take more control over their own learning and personal development. For example, Lankshear and Knobel (2003) draw attention to the pervasiveness of an 'outsider mindset' that has inhibited the development of progressive pedagogies that respect the exploratory and playful ways young people are engaging with online culture beyond the confines of formal educational contexts. As a result they explicitly advocate progressive pedagogies that respect young people's existing experience of online culture. Similarly, studies that explore the experience of young people's (Buckingham and Scanlon 2003; Facer *et al.* 2003; Sefton-Green 2004) and adults' use of computers in and beyond formal education contexts (Selwyn *et al.* 2006) advocate a pressing need to better understand and nurture learners' informal, self-directed and interest-driven practices. In this respect, it seems that the tensions emergent in university contexts are just one expression of a wider cultural shift towards an emergent culture of (self) education beyond the confines of structured curricular and accredited courses of study.

Ethnographic investigations have already advanced our understanding of this emergent culture of intrinsically motivated learning in which reputations and identities are at stake. Indeed, a growing number of studies reveal young people using new media to explore, creative, discover and connect with others who share similar interests through engagement in participatory cultures (Sefton-Green 1998; Tobin, 1998; Gee 2004; Jenkins 2006c; Ito *et al.* 2008, Buckingham, 2007). However, this emerging body of work does not always connect the insights gained with prior research in the learning sciences nor indicate how the knowledge generated might be redeployed as part of a developmental research agenda designed to empower all learners, young and old.

This book has attempted to advance this research trajectory by investigating the practices of advanced resourceful university students who enjoyed direct access to fast 'always-on' Internet connections and lived in a culture that supported the rapid diffusion of innovative practices. Given that graduate students have long histories of Internet use and live in cultures that facilitate rapid diffusion I argue that insights into how they are using the Internet promises to provide an insight into how it might be used by future generations. Further, following Olson (1994: 43) who viewed literacy 'not just as a basic set of mental skills isolated from everything else' but as the 'competence to exploit a particular set of cultural resources' and the 'knowledge and skills to exploit these resources for particular purposes', I argue that an analysis of the digitally mediated practices of graduate students can provide an insight into advanced new media literacies in action. Indeed, from a sociocultural perspective existing studies that have attempted to map out and conceptualize digital, techno or new media literacies (Gilster 1997; Tyner 1998; Snyder 1998; Kress 2003; Jenkins *et al.* 2006c) are insufficiently grounded in the study of the ways young people are now using new media in everyday life. If successful, the vignettes used in this book may serve as emblematic examples of emerging practices that can help us understanding this emergent culture of (self) education more generally.

It is also hoped that the insights offered will resonate with the experience of the reader and facilitate what Stake (2000) has described as a form of naturalistic generalization and help readers reflect upon their own changing practices. The work of conceptual development or ontological innovation (diSessa and Cobb 2004) is particularly significant in this respect. Conceptual tools that build upon existing work in the learning sciences and help us understand emergent practices can help to provide a new language that can, in turn, help us better understand, think about, describe and reflect upon emergent learning practices mediated by digital tools and resources. In turn, these conceptual tools could be used to guide further research and inform a developmental research agenda. Indeed, the social justice value of this study depends on how this empirically informed theory-building project might empower all learners, young and old, to exploit the full potential of the Internet as a learning resource. The final section provides some suggestions as to how the conceptual tools offered might facilitate this process.

Directions for further research

The question remains. How can the findings of a sociocultural investigation into the digitally mediated practices of graduate students be used to guide and inform further research and development? The work of conceptual development constitutes an important first phase. Each chapter pulled together conceptual resources that might be used to think about self-directed learning beyond the traditional university. Collectively these tools provide a framework that can empower teachers and learners to think more clearly about the challenges ahead. Nevertheless, it is important to stress that the concepts offered should also be treated with a degree of caution. Many remain rather crude tools. Most could be refined and developed through more rigorous cross-case analysis. Some remain too heavily indebted to the constructs from which they are derived and insufficiently sensitive to capture the nuances of emergent practices. In general, further conceptual development will require more fine grained and tightly focused empirical work combined with additional conceptual borrowing and synthesis. Indeed, this is essential if this research agenda is to advance with sensitivity to the subtleties of emergent practices and not remain stuck in the trap of mapping the old onto the new. In this respect, further empirically grounded conceptual development should remain a high priority.

In each chapter I attempted to develop a new language for thinking about emergent genres of learning activity by synthesizing concepts from diverse traditions. However, the development of categories and typologies builds purposefully on the central tenets of the sociocultural tradition and insights yielded by prior research in the learning sciences. As a result, the emergent genres of learning activity identified provide a robust starting point for further empirical and theoretical work. In what follows I start to map out how this research agenda might proceed.

The learner as designer

Chapter 3 builds upon insights emerging from distributed cognition theory (Clark 2003; Dennett 1996; Norman 1993; Pea 1997), multimodality theory (Kress 2003) and Vygotsky's notion of self-regulation, from the outside, to explore ways learners designed virtual desktop environments to support advanced knowledge work. Further, it illustrates how students personalize media environments evolved iteratively from *inherited* to *evolved designs* to *mindful designs*. These categories could be used to guide and focus more fine-grained investigations that explore students' design strategies. It appears particularly important to understand how some students have developed a capacity for mindful design and how this capacity empowers them to work more efficiently and effectively to achieve their purposes – whatever these might be.

The chapter suggested that shifts towards more mindful design stances are driven by authentic needs. For example, Timothy's need to complete and submit his dissertation to meet an absolute deadline appears to motivate a series of design innovations. However, other factors must be taken into account when attempting to understand why some students have developed this capacity and not others. At present, design work remains a somewhat invisible if not secretive affair. More fine-grained analytical work that explores how, why and under what circumstances students acquire a capacity for mindful design will be required to understand how this capacity evolves over time. Personal histories appear significant. Students who reap the benefits of setting aside time for self-analysis and design innovation in the past are clearly more likely to make time for conscious design work part of their weekly routine. However, design strategies have a projective component. Students, like Jim, invest time designing their personalized media ecologies when they anticipate that design work will yield long-term dividends. Other factors may be involved. This chapter also foregrounded the implications of design work for students' emotive and affective states. Further comparative work and methodological innovation is required to understand how desktop designs mediate these affective processes. Such a research agenda could help students consciously think about how to design their personalized learning environments to actively manage their intentions, purposes and priorities, from the outside, through the work of design.

If we can learn to understand this process, we will be better equipped to think about ways educators might empower all learners to consciously design personal learning environments that support advanced knowledge work. Learners who lack opportunities to compare their designs with those of friends and course mates might never become aware of the advantages to be gained. In this respect, it also seems important to develop tools that make the design strategies of advanced learners more visible. Such tools could also make the design strategies of advanced learners available for younger or less experiences learners as models of good or effective designs.

Creative appropriation

Chapter 4 builds on theoretical work by Wertsch (1998), Bahktin *et al.* (1981) and de Certeau (1988) to conceptualize how learners are *creatively appropriating* a variety of digital tools for course-related study and self-education. Interestingly, the resourcefulness of learners is often conspicuous in tool use *against the grain*, in ways not necessarily intended by the designers. This chapter also identifies a capacity to continually monitor, adapt and strategically redeploy tools as important. However, further comparative work is required to develop a more nuanced account of how students discover, learn to tinker and explore the affordances of new technologies as learning resources. The insights offered in this book suggest that students innovate to address authentic learning needs. However, prior experiences that foster a predisposition for experimentation and risk taking also appear to stimulate this process. Further, membership of cultures that help students recognize ways they might poach, pilfer and repurpose available web-based tools seems important. Prior participation in digital subcultures, like gaming and file-sharing communities, might foster a predisposition to explore, tinker and experiment. However many students – like Anastasia – appear capable of developing these capacities relatively independently. Again, this suggests a need to understand how students' values, ethical commitments and projective identities might shape the way they creatively appropriate new tools as they become available.

Developmental work that fosters a capacity for creative appropriation needs to raise awareness of the sheer variety of tools becoming available. However, more significantly, developmental work needs to help students connect with others who share similar learning needs and facilitate a culture of sharing hints, tricks and innovative practices. In turn, exercises or activities that help students consciously forecast the relative advantages and disadvantages of particular creative appropriations could help. Students need to be able to make informed choices about when to adopt and when not to adopt. Finally, a developmental agenda that aimed to empower students to exploit the full potential of the Internet needs to empower students to recognize and learn to resist strategies employed by commercial services to recruit their attention. It seems especially important to prepare younger learners to confront sophisticated marketing strategies and covert agendas that are struggling to recruit their attention in a world in which many of the traditional barriers between study space and play space have broken down.

Globally distributed funds of living knowledge

In Chapter 5 the focus shifts to explore how students are learning with others through new media. Here, conceptual tools offered by Nardi *et al*. (2002), Moll *et al*. (1997) and Edwards (2005) are used to conceptualize how and why students create, nurture and activate *distributed expertise* and exercise *relational agency* through *globally distributed funds of living knowledge*. This chapter also identifies the capacity of *knowing how to know who* and a capacity to *resist relational agency* (Edwards and Kinti 2007) and avoid dependency relationships as fundamental aspects of new media literacy.

As more and more people of all ages start to use social software to build personal and professional networks, it seems increasingly important to understand how these networks might be mobilized as a fund of living knowledge. This book has shown how university students are already using social software to leverage the distributed expertise of others to work on very specific problems and maintain close ties with distributed communities as they disperse around the world. However, further comparative and longitudinal work are required to understand how individuals cultivate, nurture and mobilize their globally distributed funds of knowledge. It seems particularly important to understanding how students are exploiting social media to negotiate critical junctures and make horizontal developments – such as major career moves. Further, it is important to understand how students are constructing their online identities and how they learn to identify others as a potential resource based upon information available online.

It is perhaps too easy to assume that all young people are rapidly developing social networking literacies as they engage in online subcultures. Even within the cohort of advanced postgraduate students studied who all lived in the same college, this did not prove to be the case. Indeed, some students like Peter had never heard of the Friendster community site at the time and later refused to open a Facebook account. Nevertheless, since this study I have interviewed students who routinely maintain multiple social software accounts for both personal and professional purposes. Some routinely upload PowerPoint presentations to SlideShare and actively seek flattering testimonials from friends and colleagues on LinkedIn. In many respects, student academic identities are on public display. Thus educators need to think carefully about the new kinds of social networking divides that are opening up and consider how to ensure all people, young and old, can be equipped with skills required to mobilize social networking applications to enhance their careers. Developmental workshops that empowered students to reflect upon, discuss and share their social networking strategies could provide a powerful way to start investigating the new opportunities. Again tools that could help students visualize their distributed personal networks and discuss how they already read and manage their online identities could help.

Learning through serious play in virtually figured worlds

Chapter 6 brings the relationship between identity and agency to the foreground. Building on the conceptual work of Bruner (1991), Gee (2004), Turkle (1997) and Holland *et al.* (1998) it argues that we need to reconceptualize personalized learning agendas in an emerging media landscape as self-making activities directed towards the actualization of a projective identity. In turn, this chapter attempts to illustrate how some advanced agentive learners are taking on professional roles and responsibilities and *bootstrapping themselves towards the actualization of their projective identities through serious play within these virtually figured worlds*. Finally, this chapter draws attention to the ways a virtually figured world might function as an *expanded space of self-authoring* that help students resist the homogenizing influence of life-world communities and navigate radically personalized lifelong learning agendas that transcend institutional boundaries.

Ito *et al.* (2008) have identified 'geeking out' as a highly significant mode of engagement among young people. In many respects I believe Chapter 6 probes further into the new possibilities for deeply committed learning and illustrates how and why young adults are now exploiting these opportunities to take on professional roles and responsibilities. As suggested, I believe this genre of (self) directed learning provides the deepest insight into the future of (self) education. It provides an insight into the emerging possibilities of pursuing lifelong learning agendas independently of any particular institution or geographical location. Significantly, Jacob, Jim and Clinton, the three students who seemed to become deeply and passionately engaged in self-directed learning activities had made commitments to a particular projective identity before they became participants in this study. Moreover, interviews revealed that these students' projective identities were forged in their teenage years through participation in lifeworld activities together with online activities. Therefore, we still need to understand the degree to which learners' identities are forged dialectically and dialogically through participation in both lifeworld and virtually figured worlds over time. Longitudinal studies that follow learners as they negotiate critical junctures and move across institutional boundaries could reveal important insights into this process. For example, it would be interesting to explore what became of Heather and Isaac as they ventured into their adult lives. We could then understand how the identities they acquired as teen editors through a form of serious play continued to shape their developmental trajectories over time. Similarly, it would be extremely interesting to revisit the likes of Clinton, Jacob and Jim in an attempt to understand the degree to which their participation in their respective virtually figured worlds empowered them actualize their respective projective identities. The case of Jim suggests it would be particularly interesting to explore how identity work in virtually figured worlds might empower an individual to get out of rut and back into a groove.

Developmental activities could also be devised to help students recognize the various ways they already learn through serious play in virtually figured worlds. If, as I have suggested, opportunities of learning through intrinsically motivated self-directed engagement in online culture are expanding, we need to help young people understand how they might best exploit these opportunities to realize their potential. Young people need to understand how their virtually figured worlds might shape their sense of self and community, their sense of who they are and who they might become. They need to understand how *history in laptop* might canalize their personal development and how their virtually figured worlds might function as an *expanded space of self-authoring* and empower them to negotiate critical junctures as they progress through life.

Towards a developmental research agenda

In the mid-term, it is hoped that the tools offered in this book could provide the basis of a developmental research agenda. Indeed, if the conceptual tools offered help readers reflect upon their own practices, identify tensions and adopt a more mindful stance towards their own virtually figured worlds it has already served a developmental function. However, in the long term developmental workshops, purposefully designed for groups of students could accelerate this process.

A tradition known as Developmental Work Research (DWR), purposefully aims to empower groups of workers to reflect upon and become more conscious of the tensions and contradictions regarding development among teams in workplace settings. (Engeström 2001, 2005; Engeström *et al.* 1997; Engeström and Middleton 1996). This tradition uses an approach known as the 'mirror method' is used to help teams become more conscious of the mediated nature of their own collective activities (Engeström 2007). Following a period of observation, researchers typically create a collection of diagrams that helps participants visualize the activity systems in which they participate. These conceptual tools are then used to facilitate reflective discussion among team members. The aim is to empower all team members to become more conscious of the tensions, contradictions and object-motives that define the activity systems in which they participate. In this respect DWR aims to raise group awareness of their own predicament and facilitate an expansive transformation that will empower the team to achieve its full potential. In contrast to strategic decisions imposed on the team or organization from the top down by senior management, this bottom-up approach ensures that any transformative actions that emerge are grounded in a shared recognition of the tensions retarding collective progress and thereby increases the possibility of achieving deep and sustainable change.

I can imagine workshops that used a modified version of the mirror method could help small groups of students identify and analyse the tensions inherent in their own digitally mediated practices. Activities could then be devised to help students mindfully redesign their personalized learning environments, discuss how they already creatively appropriate web-based tools and resources for study and consciously cultivate, nurture and mobilize globally distributed funds of living knowledge. Finally, activities could be devised to help students reflect upon their own sense of self and community and explore new opportunities to learn through serious play in virtually figured worlds. The details need to be worked out. However, in all cases the aim would be to empower students to become more mindful of the ways their engagement with online culture mediates their own learning and personal development.

Existing formats, such as career guidance workshops that encourage students to reflect upon and discuss career possibilities, suggest a model that could be effectively used within a university context. In each case, the workshop leader would need to devise activities and tools that encouraged students to share, discuss and reflect upon existing practices. Critically, such an approach would need to respect students' existing practices, help students share and reflect upon these practices and adopt a more mindful stance towards the design and configuration of their own virtually figured worlds. Such an approach works with the emerging trends. If the general conclusions of this book are accurate and we are indeed witnessing the decentring of the traditional university – such an approach may prove the only effective way to ensure that students are fully prepared to negotiate the challenges of participatory cultures.

In the long term, educationalists need to consider how the knowledge produced through investigations focused on the practices of advanced resourceful students studying at well-established universities could be used as part of a wider developmental agenda. Indeed, the 'social justice' value of the current study can only be appreciated when one starts to consider how the findings might inform developmental research aimed at teaching less capable (and less privileged) groups how to exploit the full potential of the Internet as a learning resource. This challenge appears particularly important in a world in which a fast, always-on wireless Internet connection, like the telephone, radio and television before it, seems set to become part of the fabric of everyday life for the vast majority of people living in advanced industrial societies and much of the developing world.

Appendix: data collection strategy and methods

Data collection involved the use of multiple qualitative methods. The procedure started with a series of informal conversations. Each participant who consented to take part in the study completed a pre-interview questionnaire at which time some notes were made about the arrangement of their computers and other resources ready-to-hand in their study rooms. Each then participated in an interview followed by a period of observation and short stimulated response sessions conducted at their computer. Screen shots were captured at this time.

Data collection continued, after the initial analysis, with follow-up interviews and e-mail correspondence. Some of the interviews also prompted retrospective use of tools or websites participants had demonstrated or a period of participant observation in an online affinity space discussed during interview. At this time, further on-screen data could be captured. As stipulated, no data source was excluded that might shed light on the practices observed. A breakdown of the purpose and use of each data collection method is now discussed in turn.

Informal conversations

Informal conversations helped identify potential participants for the study. These invariably took place in social spaces such as the college dining room or bar and often began spontaneously. These conversations provided a rich source of inspiration and a means to facilitate the generation of hypotheses. Only students who seemed willing to participate in in-depth interviews and stimulated response sessions whilst working at their computer in their study rooms were considered as potential recruits. A certain degree of frankness and honesty also remained important as a criteria in the selection process.

Whilst comparisons with cohorts of Internet users in other studies are made, it is important to stress that the group cannot be considered representative of the student population in the university or the college. It remained essential to respect the specificity of each case and attempt to understand how each student's circumstances might prove significant when attempting to understand individual styles of computer use.

Pre-interview questionnaire

The pre-interview questionnaire was designed to capture information that could inform subsequent interviews and observations. Questions were posed with the use of tick boxes, Likert scale style responses and open-ended response boxes. Besides basic demographic information, topics covered included: ownership of personal computing; estimates of time spent using the computer; questions relating to tools used for different types of task (subscriptions to news groups, listservs, RSS feeds, blogs and wikis); experience of online activities (games, file sharing, shopping, chat, banking, etc.); and the use of CMC tools (e-mail, chat, telephony, text messages, etc.). The questionnaire, designed to take approximately twenty minutes to complete, also included more open-ended questions gauging general attitudes towards computers. Little of the questionnaire data is used in the final analysis. It abstracted aspects of computer use from situated practice and compromised the principle of *following the learner*. However, since it provided the only structured source of data, it proved useful for organizational purposes; for comparing the group (to populations sampled in other studies) and for throwing out interesting points that could be explored in interviews and used to focus stimulated response sessions. A short interview was held upon completion that picked up on any interesting or unexpected responses in the questionnaire.

Observation notes

Observation notes were taken about the layout and arrangement of the study room and non-digital resources that students had placed 'ready-to-hand' whilst the students completed the pre-interview questionnaire. In some cases, a photograph or short sketch was also taken of the area immediately around the computer with a view to developing a chapter on the ecology of the offline study environment (not included in the final draft). Nevertheless, this data source provided contextual information that proved helpful for understanding certain aspects of practices such as students' relative dependence on digital and non-digital resources.

Stimulated response

Stimulated response sessions provided a rich data source and provided the most direct insight into digitally mediated practice. The method is similar to the 'think aloud protocol' or 'cognitive walkthroughs' used in controlled environments by computer-human interaction researchers to evaluate interface design (Preece *et al.* 2002: 365–368; Rikard and Langley 1995). However, Vygotsky's genetic method provided the model and a source of inspiration. In all cases, the aim was to understand how and why learners actively appropriated and used digital tools and resources to mediate their own learning activities.

The method was used to investigate naturalistic practices, following the learner, as he or she engaged in authentic goal-directed tasks. Crucially, students' own needs and priorities led the stimulated response sessions. Consequently, the walkthrough was not restricted to a particular tool and no assumptions were made about the goal or end point of the practice observed in advance. Nevertheless, following the logic of theoretic sampling instances in which learners appeared to appropriate a new tool (or combination of tools) to overcome a tension, contradiction or escape a double bind situation proved especially interesting. Similarly, instances in which students used a tool *against the grain* (in ways not intended by the designers) or instances in which students refrained from using the full functionality of a tool proved of great interest. In these instances, the agency of the learner became conspicuous.

The data generated through this method were directly stimulated by on-screen activity and thus directly related to situated practice. In this sense, they provided 'raw' data that were later used to reconstruct a number of illustrative vignettes.

Interestingly, the method itself appeared to stimulate a form of reflective practice and contributed to insights about the degree to which students were conscious or *mindful* of the ways access to digital technologies had started to mediate their own learning strategies (see Chapter 3 *Towards a theory of mindful design*). Indeed, in the case of Jim and Ardash (who both became heavily involved in the study and began e-mailing observations about strategies they had innovated) the initial sessions appeared to inspire a sustained period of self-reflection on their own evolving practice. This suggests that the method could be used as part of a developmental research agenda.

In-depth interviews

All participants took part in one or more in-depth interviews about their use of computers and the Internet. Questions in the first section included: 'When did you first start using computers?'; 'What did you use them for?', and 'Do you have any hobbies or interests that involve the use of computer software?' These proved important for understanding individuals' enculturation into computer use and their relative experience of participation in online culture. Questions in the second section included: 'Can you explain how you came to study at Oxford?'; 'Why did you choose to study [x]?', and 'What kind of career are you considering and why?' These proved important for understanding personal life trajectories and priorities of each student. A third section focused on the design of their physical and virtual working environment. This section supplied additional contextual information about the ecology of the working environment and their relative dependence on digital versus non-digital tools and resources.

The fourth section did not follow a predefined structure. It made use of an interview prompt sheet that grouped questions under subheadings loosely corresponding to emergent themes. This format allowed for a more flexible interview style. Indeed, it evolved throughout the study to provide a set of prompts that could be used to pick up and explore issues uncovered during stimulated response sessions. No single interview followed a set format. The prompt sheet simply provided a resource that could be used to probe various points that might emerge during an ongoing conversation led by the informant. In short, the use of themed 'points to explore' lists facilitated a shift between a research led 'respondent interview' and a student led 'informant' interview (Robson 2002: 271). These themed 'points to explore' lists were updated or revised following each interview.

Interviews were recorded on audiotape and later on a digital Dictaphone, then summarized and transcribed. Initial interviews were transcribed in full. However, the length of each interview grew as the study progressed and the more in-depth cases studies (Ardash, Timothy, Jim, Edina and Miss Lullaby, Jacob) involved multiple interviews. These were summarized and the most pertinent sections were transcribed in full.

Follow up interviews and e-mail correspondence

Eight students (Jim, Ardash, Jacob, Edina, Miss Lullaby, Tim, Katrina and ZeroGBoy) participated in subsequent follow-up interviews after preliminary data analysis. These proved useful as a means to clarify or probe interesting points that emerged. When expedient, these were conducted on a face-to-face basis. However, these were not always recorded. Further, several students were no longer living in the immediate vicinity or (in one case) were away conducting field work by the time data had been transcribed and analysed. In these cases, certain points were probed further via e-mail correspondence. This strategy facilitated the posing of specific questions relating to particular data items (typically an extract of recorded speech) and consequently elicited focused responses. In addition, several students who had become very involved occasionally e-mailed interesting comments or observations following reflections on their own practice. These e-mails were not intentionally solicited. However, they were considered a legitimate and valuable data source.

Retrospective virtual ethnography

Retrospective virtual ethnography' resembles an approach recommended by Hine (2000) who spent time as a participant observer in various online spaces recording and documenting on-screen data to investigate a media event. Hine uses the term virtual ethnography to describe a methodology she developed for researching the online 'media event' that erupted on the Internet during the controversial case of British nanny, Louise Woodward, who was put on trial for the murder of a baby in her care. This method involved spending time as a participant observer in online spaces, including websites, newsgroups, blogs and online discussion forums, recording and documenting online data. She also conducted e-mail interviews with selected participants.

In this study short periods of virtual ethnography were motivated by a need to gain a better understanding of the online services and online groups students had discussed in interviews. Participation helped to develop further insights into why and how participants were making use of online resources. It also provided further opportunities to take screen shots of tools, sites and user generated content.

As a method it evolved to account for the emergence of Web 2.0. During interviews and stimulated response sessions, students often discussed or demonstrated their use of a particular tool or participation in an online group. However, it was not always possible to develop a full understanding of the utility of the tool, service or online group at this time. Consequently, it proved expedient to experiment with tools and, in some cases, join and start to participate in online groups after the session. Following early case studies I found myself watching academic podcasts on YouTube, comparing political speeches on C-SPAN and using Amazon.com's 'Search Inside Me' tool for finding a missing reference. Later I joined and participated in a number of online groups including: Aids India, Chessbase and Vegidate.com to gain a fuller understanding of the utility and participatory practices afforded by each group. Similarly, following interviews I started to use MSN Messenger, opened a Friendster community account and by the end of the study I had become an member of multiple online affinity groups and an active participant in Facebook.

Retrospective virtual ethnography promises to become an important and necessary tool for researching emerging learning strategies now Web 2.0 has come to maturity. It has the potential to provide an insider perspective of the dynamics of an online group conceived as an activity system as opposed to a semiotic space. In this respect, it promises to provide a more in-depth insight into the ways students are starting to engage with participatory culture. Importantly, it sensitizes one to the less conspicuous modes of participation that are rarely picked up by researchers who rely too extensively on screen-based content. Indeed, this method becomes even more useful for understanding emergent learning practices mediated by a variety of Web 2.0 technologies. In a follow-up study focused specifically on Web 2.0 technologies I found myself using the social bookmarking tool Stumble Upon, spent time investigating Deviant Art, Flickr and Live Leak following interviews with students who used these tools.

Notes

Introduction

1 28 October 1943 to the House of Commons (meeting in the House of Lords).

1 From the culture industry to participatory culture

1 In the *Culture Industry Reconsidered* Adorno (1999 [1975]) provides a lucid theoretical treatment of the genesis of the culture industry trope that was first used in the seminal treatise *Dialectic of Enlightenment* (Adorno and Horkheimer 1972 [1947]).

2 The essay reprinted in *The Media Studies* (2004) is an abridged version of Enzensberger's (1974) *The Consciousness Industry: on Literature, Politics and the Media*, ed. Michael Roloff (New York: Seabury). It was originally published as 'Baukasten zu einer, Theorie der Medien' in *Kursbuch* 18 (1971) in German and translated by Stuart Hood for the *New Left Review*.

3 Enzensberger's 1974 critique is aimed more directly at the likes of George Orwell's 'bogey of a monolithic consciousness industry' that Enzensberger claims 'derives from a view of the media which is undialectical and obsolete' (p. 70). Nevertheless, he adds, 'nor are the works of Adorno and Horkheimer free from the nostalgia of bourgeoisie media' (p. 70).

4 Raymond Williams, the son of a railway worker and a committed socialist, is generally regarded as the forefather of The Birmingham School for Cultural Studies (Clarke 1993; Cohen 2005; Hall and Jefferson 1976; Hebdige 2005; McRobbie 1975; Willis 2005; Young 2005). These theorists tend to adopt an interdisciplinary approach and weave together elements from post-Marxist, post-structuralist, feminist and post-colonial theory in an attempt to interpret the findings of ethnographic investigations focused on marginalized groups. The term 'site of struggle' is closely associated with Williams' (1961, 1983) pioneering work.

5 Henry Jenkins was the founder and director of the Comparative Media Studies Programme at MIT. In 2009 he moved to the University of Southern California and become the Provost Professor at the Annenberg School of Communication, Journalism and Cinematic Arts.

6 Ad-busting refers to the practice of reworking or recycling the iconography and symbolism of global corporations to produce satirical 'mash-ups' or politically motivated anti-corporate adverts. Jenkins (2006b: 137) describes ad-busting as a

practice that 'borrows iconography from Madison Avenue to deliver an anti-corporate or anti-consumerist message'. The ads are typically broadcast over the Internet or used by anti-capitalist campaigners.

7 I continued to interview and hold focus group discussions with students about their use of emerging technologies. More recent work explores the way social media has impacted upon students' sense of self and community.

2 Cognitive anthropology on the Cyberian frontier

1 Cole (1996: pp. 7–37) constructs the tradition in broader terms under the umbrella term 'cultural psychology' that has its origins in *Völkerpsychologie* or a second psychology that Wilheim Wundt (1921) argued was required to understand how culture entered into higher psychological processes. From this perspective 'sociocultural' and 'activity theory' are regarded as later developments.

2 The New London Group consisted of a group scholars from various disciplinary backgrounds who shared an interest in literacy: Courtney Cazden (classroom discourse and language learning in multi-lingual contexts); Bill Cope (changing discourses of the work place); Norman Fairclough and James Paul Gee (language and mind); Mary Kalantzis (citizenship education); Gunter Kress (language, learning, semiotics and visual literacy); Allan Luke (sociological approaches to the teaching of reading and writing); Carmen Luke (feminist pedagogy); Sarah Michels (classroom learning in urban settings); and Martin Nakata (literacy in indigenous communities).

3 The learner as designer

1 *Sine qua non* or *conditio sine qua non* was originally a Latin legal term for 'without which it could not be' according to the Wikipedia article on the term.

2 MRI (Magnetic Resonance Imaging) has been used since the beginning of the 1980s.

3 Burke's dramaturgical metaphor schematized as a dramatic pentad in the *Grammar of Motives* (Burke 1969) conceptualizes purposeful action using five elements: act, scene, agent, agency and purpose. It is recommended by Wertsch (1998) as a powerful conceptual schema for understanding tool-mediated action in particular sociocultural contexts.

4 Creative appropriation, new media and self-education

1 For Vygotsky (1986), learning involves a dialectic movement between *spontaneous* and *scientific* concepts towards the formation of a *mature* concepts. Spontaneous concepts tend to precede the acquisition of the scientific concept that later synthesize into a mature concept. For example, as infants most of us develop an intuitive, pre-verbal or *spontaneous* notion of the concept 'brother' before we learn to say the word-concept 'brother'. However, once acquired, the *scientific* word-concept defines and organizes the vague and somewhat foggy spontaneous concept. The synthesis of the two is the *mature* concept 'brother'. Overtime, the *mature* concept acquires a more precise meaning as it becomes assimilated into a language system consisting of related concepts (such as father sister, uncle, cousin, sister, etc.).

5 Globally distributed funds of living knowledge

1 After leaving Oxford, Miss Lullaby took a job working for an NGO in Texas. The job involved investigating the backgrounds of inmates on death row in an attempt to find exonerating evidence that might be used by attorneys to overturn sentences or more typically to stall execution dates.

6 Learning through serious play in virtually figured worlds

1 A flirt bot is a term used to describe an artificially intelligent agent that pretends to be a female character and flirts with people who attempt to talk to it.
2 The concept of a psycho-social moratorium was originally developed by Erik Erikson in *Childhood and Society* (1963 [1950]) in an attempt to understand the emergence of adolescent subcultures in the 1950s.

Bibliography

Abbott, C. (2002), 'Writing the Visual: The Use of Graphic Symbols in Onscreen Texts', in I. Snyder (ed.), *Silicon Literacies: Communication, Innovation and Education in Electronic Age*, Routledge, London, pp. 31–46.

Adorno, T.W. (1999 [1975]), 'Culture Industry Reconsidered', in P. Marris and S. Thornham (eds), *Media Studies: A Reader*, Edinburgh University Press, Edinburgh, pp. 31–37.

Adorno, T.W. and Horkheimer, M. (1972 [1947]), *Dialectic of Enlightenment*, Verso, London.

Austin, J.L., Urmson, J.O. and Sbisáa, M. (1978), *How to Do Things with Words: The William James Lectures Delivered at Harvard University in 1955*, second edition, Oxford University Press, Oxford.

Bakhtin, M.M. (1981), *The Dialogic Imagination: Four Essays*, trans. and ed. by M. Holquist, V. Liapunov and K. Brostrom, University of Texas Press, Austin, TX.

Barnsley, G., Shariff, P.W. and Barnsley, G. (2004), 'Literacy Practice in Cyber-space', in C. Durrant and C. Beavis (eds), *P(ICT)ures of English: Teachers, Learners and Technology*, Wakefield Press, Kent Town, SA.

Bateson, G. (1978), 'The Birth of a Matrix or Double Bind and Epistemology', in M.M. Berger (ed.), *Beyond the Double Bind*, Brunner/Mazel, New York, pp. 39–64.

—— (2000), *Steps to an Ecology of Mind*, University of Chicago Press, Chicago/ London.

Battelle, J. (2006), *The Search: How Google and Its Rivals Rewrote the Rules of Business and Transformed Our Culture*, revised edition, Nicholas Brealey, London.

Beavis, C. (2002), 'Reading, Writing and Role-Playing Computer Games', in I. Snyder (ed.), *Silicon Literacies: Communication, Innovation and Education in the Electronic Age*, Routledge, London, pp. 47–61.

Bergson, H. (1983 [1911]), *Creative Evolution*, H. Holt, New York.

Biggs, J. (1988), 'The Role of Metacognition in Enhancing Learning', *Australian Journal of Education*, 32(2): 127–138.

Blustein, H., Goldstein, P. and Lozier, G. (1999), 'Assessing the New Competitive Landscape', in R.N. Katz (ed.), *Dancing with the Devil: Information Technology and the New Competition in Higher Education*, Jossey-Bass Publishers, San Francisco, CA.

Bourdieu, P. (1977), *Outline of a Theory of Practice*, trans. R. Nice, Cambridge University Press, Cambridge.

Bruner, J.S. (1986), *Actual Minds, Possible Worlds*, Harvard University Press, Cambridge, MA.

—— (1991), 'Self-Making and World-Making', *Journal of Aesthetic Education*, 25(1): 67–78.

—— (1996), *The Culture of Education*, Harvard University Press, Cambridge MA.

Buckingham D. (2007), *Beyond Technology: Children's Learning in the Age of Digital Culture*, Polity Press, Cambridge.

Buckingham, D. and Scanlon, M. (2003), *Education, Entertainment and Learning in the Home*, Open University Press, Buckingham.

Burke, K. (1969), *A Grammar of Motives*, University of California Press, Berkeley, CA.

Burton, R. and Brown, J.S. (1988), 'Skiing as a Model of Instruction', in B. Rogoff and J. Lave (eds), *Everyday Cognition: Development in Social Context*, Harvard University Press, Cambridge, MA, pp. 139–150.

Castells, M. (2000), *The Rise of the Network Society*, second edition, Blackwell, Oxford.

Castronova, E. (2001), 'Virtual Worlds: A First-Hand Account of Market and Society on the Cyberian Frontier', *CESifo Working Paper series No, 618*. Online. Available at: ssrn.com/abstract=294828 (accessed 8 November 2004).

Clark, A. (2003), *Natural-Born Cyborgs*, Oxford University Press, New York.

Clarke, J. (1993), 'Subcultures, Cultures and Class', in S. Hall and T. Jefferson (eds), *Resistance through Rituals*, Routledge, London/New York, pp. 99–102.

Coffield, F. (2000), *The Necessity of Informal Learning*, Policy Press, Bristol.

Cohen, P. (2005), 'Subcultural Conflict and Work-Class Community', in K. Gelder (ed.), *The Subcultures Reader*, second edition, Routledge, London/New York, pp. 90–99.

Cole, M. (1985), 'The Zone of Proximal Development: Where Culture and Cognition Create Each Other', in J.V. Wertsch (ed.), *Culture, Communication, and Cognition: Vygotskian Perspectives*, Cambridge University Press, Cambridge, pp. 379–390.

—— (1996), *Cultural Psychology: A Once and Future Discipline*, Belknap Press of Harvard University Press, Cambridge, MA/London.

Cole, M. and Derry, J. (2005), 'We Have Met Technology and it is Us', in R.J. Sternberg and D.D. Preiss (eds), *Intelligence and Technology: Impact of Tools on the Nature and Development of Human Abilities*, Lawrence Erlbaum Associates, Mahwah, NJ.

Cole, M. and Wertsch, J.V. (1996), 'Beyond the Individual-Social Antinomy in Discussions of Piaget and Vygotsky', *Human Development*, 39(2): 250–256.

Crook, C. (2007), 'Learning Science and Learning Technology: Finding a Place for Cultural Psychology', in J.D.M. Underwood and J. Dockrell (eds), *Learning Through Digital Technologies*, British Psychological Society, London, pp. 1–17.

Crook, C. and Light, P. (2002), 'Virtual Society and the Cultural Practice of Study', in S. Woolgar (ed.), *Virtual Society?: Technology, Cyberbole, Reality*, Oxford University Press, Oxford, pp. 153–175.

Cuban, L. (2001), *Oversold and Underused: Computers in the Classroom*, Harvard University Press, Cambridge, MA/London.

D'Andrade, R.G. (1995), *The Development of Cognitive Anthropology*, Cambridge University Press, Cambridge.

Daniels, H. (2005), *An Introduction to Vygotsky*, second edition, Routledge, London.

Davydov, V.V. and Radzikhovskii, L.A. (1985), 'Vygotsky's Theory and the Activity-Orientated Approach in Psychology', in J.V. Wertsch (ed.), *Culture, Communication, and Cognition: Vygotskian Perspectives*, Cambridge University Press, Cambridge.

de Certeau, M. (1988), *The Practice of Everyday Life*, second edition, University of California Press, Berkeley, CA/London.

Dennett, D.C. (1996), *Kinds of Minds: Towards an Understanding of Consciousness*, Weidenfeld & Nicolson, London.

Dewey, J. (1998), *How We Think: A Restatement of the Relation of Reflective Thinking To*, revised and expanded edition, Houghton Mifflin, Boston, MA.

diSessa, A. and Cobb, P. (2004), 'Ontological Innovation and the Role of Theory in Design Experiments', *Journal of the Learning Sciences*, 13(1): 77–103.

Durrant, C. and Beavis, C. (eds) (2004), *P(ICT)ures of English: Teachers, Learners and Technology*, Wakefield Press, Kent Town, SA.

Edwards, A. (2005), 'Relational Agency: Learning to be a Resourceful Practitioner', *International Journal of Educational Research*, 43(3): 168–182.

—— (2010) *Being an Expert Professional Practitioner: The Relational Turn in Expertise*, Springer, Dordecht.

—— (in press), 'Learning How to Know Who: Professional Learning for Expansive Practice between Organisations', in S.R. Ludvigsen, A. Lund, I. Rasmussen and R. Säljö (eds), *Learning Across Sites: New Tools, Infrastructures and Practices*, Routledge, Abingdon.

Edwards, A. and D'Arcy, C. (2004), 'Relational Agency and Disposition in Socio-cultural Accounts of Learning to Teach', *Educational Review*, 56(2): 147–155.

Edwards, A. and Kinti, I. (2007), *Resisting Relational Agency: Working on the Boundaries of Schooling*, EARLI Conference, Budapest (refereed). Online. Available at: www.education.ox.ac.uk/uploaded/OSAT/ EARLIedwardspaper2. doc.

Ellis, R. and Goodyear P. (2010), *Students' Experiences of E-Learning in Higher Education: The Ecology of Sustainable Innovation*, Routledge, Abingdon/New York.

Engeström, Y. (1987), *Learning by Expanding*, Orienta-Konsultit Oy, Helsinki.

—— (1996), 'Development as Breaking Away and Opening Up: A Challenge to Vygotsky and Piaget', *Swiss Journal of Psychology*, 55: 126–132.

—— (1999), 'Activity Theory and Individual and Social Transformation', in R. Miettinen and R.-L. Punamèaki-Gitai (eds), *Perspectives on Activity Theory*, Cambridge University Press, Cambridge/New York, pp. 19–38.

—— (2001), 'Expansive Learning at Work: Toward an Activity-Theoretical Reconceptualisation', *Journal of Education and Work*, 14(1): 133–156.

—— (2005), 'Knotworking to Create Collaborative Intentionality Capital in Fluid Organisational Fields', *Advances in Interdisciplinary Studies of Work Teams*, 11: 307–336.

—— (2007), 'Putting Vygotsky to Work: The Change Laboratory as an Application of Double Stimulation', in H. Daniels, M. Cole and J.V. Wertsch (eds), *The Cambridge Companion to Vygotsky*, Cambridge University Press, Cambridge/ New York, pp. 363–382.

Engeström, Y. and Middleton, D. (1996), *Cognition and Communication at Work*, Cambridge University Press, Cambridge.

Engeström, Y., Miettinen, R. and Punamèaki-Gitai, R.-L. (eds) (1999), *Perspectives on Activity Theory*, Cambridge University Press, Cambridge/New York.

Engeström, Y., Brown, C.L., Christopher, C. and Gregory, J. (1997), 'Coordination, Cooperation, and Communication in the Courts: Expansive Transitions in Legal Work', in M. Cole, Y. Engeström and O.A. Vasquez (eds), *Mind, Culture, and Activity: Seminal Papers from the Laboratory of Comparative Human Cognition*, Cambridge University Press, Cambridge, pp. 369–387.

Enzensberger, H.M. (2004 [1974]), 'Constituents of a theory of the media', in *Media Studies: A Reader*, edited by P. Marris and S. Thornham, second edition, New York University Press, New York, pp. 68–91.

Erikson, E.H. (1963 [1950]), *Childhood and Society*, second edition, Norton, New York.

Facer, K., Furlong, J., Sutherland, R. and Furlong, R. (2003), *Screenplay: Children and Computing in the Home*, RoutledgeFalmer, London.

Forman, E. and Cazden, C.B. (1985), 'Exploring Vygotskian Perspectives in Education: The Cognitive Value of Peer Interaction', in J.V. Wertsch (ed.), *Culture, Communication, and Cognition: Vygotskian Perspectives*, Cambridge University Press, Cambridge, pp. 323–347.

Francis, R.J. (2008), '*The Predicament of the Learner in the New Media Age: An Investigation into the Implications of Media Change for Learning*', DPhil thesis, University of Oxford, Oxford. Online. Available at: http://ora.ouls.ox.ac.uk/objects/uuid:0cbd0185-c7ed-4306-b34e-993acd125e96.

Freire, P. (1985), *Pedagogy of the Oppressed*, Penguin, Harmondsworth.

Gee, J.P. (1996), *Social Linguistics and Literacies: Ideology in Discourses*, second edition, Routledge, London/New York.

—— (2000a), 'The New Literacy Studies: From "Socially Situated" To the Work of of the Social', in D. Barton, M. Hamilton and R. Ivanic (eds), *Situating Literacies: Reading and Writing in Context*, Routledge, London, pp. 180–196.

—— (2000b), 'Teenagers in New Times: A New Literacy Studies Perspective', *Journal of Adolescent and Adult Literacy*, 43(5): 412–423.

—— (2003), *What Video Games Have to Teach Us About Learning and Literacy*, Palgrave Macmillan, New York/Basingstoke.

—— (2004), *Situated Language and Learning: A Critique of Traditional Schooling*, Routledge, New York/London.

Giddens, A. (1984), *The Constitution of Society: Outline of the Theory of Structuration*, Polity Press, Cambridge.

Gilster, P. (1997), *Digital Literacy*, Wiley, New York/Chichester.

Goldhaber, M. (1996), *Principles of the New Economy*. Online. Available at: www.well.com/user/mgoldh/principles.html [accessed 15 November 2005].

—— (1997), 'The Attention Economy and the Net', *First Monday*, 2(4). Online. Available at: http://firstmonday.org/htbin/cgiwrap/bin/ojs/index.php/fm/article/ view/519/440 [accessed 27 September 2005].

González, N., Moll, L.C. and Amanti, C. (2004), *Funds of Knowledge: Theorizing Practices in Households, Communities, and Classrooms*, Lawrence Erlbaum, Mahwah, NJ.

Green, H., Facer, K., Rudd, T., Dillon, P. and Humpreys, P. (2005), *Personalisation and Digital Technologies*, Futurelab, Bristol. Online. Available at: www.futurelab.org.uk/resources/documents/opening_education/Personalisation_report.pdf [accessed 8 June 2005].

Hall, S. and Jefferson, T. (1976), *Resistance Through Rituals: Youth Subcultures in Post-War Britain*, Hutchinson, London.

Hawisher G. and Self, C. (1998), 'Reflections on Computers and Composition Studies at the Century's End', in I. Snyder (ed.), *Page to Screen: Taking Literacy into the Electronic Era*, London, Routledge, pp. 3–19.

Hebdige, D. (2005), 'Subculture: The Meaning of Style', in K. Gelder (ed.), *The Subcultures Reader*, second edition, Routledge, London/New York.

Hine, C. (2000), *Virtual Ethnography*, SAGE, London.

Holland, D.C., Skinner, D., Lachicotte Jr., W. and Cain, C. (1998), *Identity and Agency in Cultural Worlds*, Harvard University Press, Cambridge, MA.

Hutchins, E. (1995a), *Cognition in the Wild*, MIT Press, Cambridge, MA/London.

—— (1995b), 'How a Cockpit Remembers Its Speeds', *Cognitive Science*, 19: 265–288.

—— (1997), 'Mediation and Automation', in M. Cole, Y. Engeström and O.A. Vasquez (eds), *Mind, Culture, and Activity: Seminal Papers from the Laboratory of Comparative Human Cognition*, Cambridge University Press, Cambridge, pp. 338–353.

Ilyenkov, E.V. (1977), 'The Concept of the Ideal', in *Philosophy in the U.S.S.R: Problems of Dialectical Materialism*, Progress Publishers, Moscow.

—— (1982), *The Dialectics of the Abstract and the Concrete in Marx's 'Capital'*, Progress Publishers, Moscow.

Ito, M., Horst, H., Bittanti, M., Boyd, D., Herr-Stephenson, B., Lange, P.G., Pascoe, C.J. and Robinson, L. (2008), *Living and Learning with New Media: Summary of Findings from the Digital Youth Project*, The MacArthur Foundation. Online. Available at: http://digitalyouth.ischool.berkeley.edu/files/report/digitalyouth-WhitePaper.pdf [accessed 5 May 2009].

Jenkins, H. (1992), *Textual Poachers: Television Fans and Participatory Culture*, Routledge, New York.

—— (2006a), *Convergence Culture: When Old and New Media Collide*, New York University Press, New York.

—— (2006b), *Fans, Bloggers, and Gamers: Exploring Participatory Culture*, New York University Press, New York.

—— (2006c), 'Why Heather Can Write', in *Convergence Culture: When Old and New Media Collide*, New York University Press, New York, pp. 169–205.

Jenkins, H., Purushotma, R., Clinton, K., Weigel, M. and Robinson, A. (2006), *Confronting the Challenges of Participatory Culture: Media Education for the 21st Century*, Comparative Media Studies Program at the Massachusetts Institute of Technology, Cambridge, MA. Online. Available at: www.projectnml.org/files/working/NMLWhitePaper.pdf [accessed 10 November 2006].

Jones, S. (2002), *The Internet Goes to College: How Students Are Living in the Future with Today's Technology*, Pew Internet and American Life Project. Online. Available at: www.pewinternet.org/Reports/2002/The-Internet-Goes-to-College. aspx [accessed 10 September 2006].

Joyce, M. (1998), 'New Stories for New Readers: Contour, Coherence and Constructive Hypertext', in I. Snyder (ed.), *Page to Screen: Taking Literacy into the Electronic Era*, London, Routledge, pp. 163–182.

Kist, W. (2005), *New Literacies in Action: Teaching and Learning in Multiple Media*, Teachers College Press, New York.

Kozulin, A. (2003), 'Psychological Tools and Mediated Learning', in A. Kozulin, B. Gindis, V.S. Ageyev and S.M. Miller (eds), *Vygotsky's Educational Theory in Cultural Context*, Cambridge University Press, Cambridge, pp. 15–38.

Knobel, M., Lankshear, C., Honan, E. and Crawford, J. (1998), 'The Wired World of Second Language Education', in I. Snyder (ed.), *Page to Screen: Taking Literacy into the Electronic Era*, Routledge, London, pp. 21–52.

Kreijns, K., Kirschner, P.A. and Jochems, W. (2003), 'Identifying the Pitfalls for Social Interaction in Computer-Supported Collaborative Learning Environments: A Review of the Research', *Computers in Human Behaviour*, 19(3): 335–353.

Kress, G. (2000), 'Multimodality', in B. Cope, M. Kalantzis and New London Group (eds), *Multiliteracies: Literacy Learning and the Design of Social Futures*, Routledge, London, pp. 182–202.

—— (2003), *Literacy in the New Media Age*, Routledge, London.

Kubrick, S. (1968), *2001: A Space Odyssey*, MGM (producer), UK.

Lankshear, C. and Knobel, M. (2003), *New Literacies: Changing Knowledge and Classroom Learning*, Open University Press, Buckingham.

Laurillard, D. (2002), *Rethinking University Teaching: A Conversational Framework for the Effective Use of Learning Technologies*, RoutledgeFalmer, London.

Lave, J. and Wenger, E. (1991), *Situated Learning: Legitimate Peripheral Participation*, Cambridge University Press, Cambridge.

Lave, J., Murtaugh, M. and Rocha, O. (1984), 'The Dialectic of Arithmetic in Grocery Shopping', in B. Rogoff and J. Lave (eds), *Everyday Cognition: Its Development in Social Context*, Harvard University Press, Cambridge, MA, pp. 67–94.

Lenhart, A., Simon, M. and Graziano, M. (2001), *The Internet and Education*, Pew Internet and American Life Project. Online. Available at: www.pewinternet.org/Reports/2001/The-Internet-and-Education.aspx [accessed 7 May 2006].

Leont'ev, A.N. (1979), *Activity, Consciousness and Personality*, Prentice-Hall, Upper Saddle River, NJ. Online. Available at: www.marx.org/archive/leontev/works/1978/index.htm [accessed 4 July 2005].

Lévy, P. (1997), *Collective Intelligence: Mankind's Emerging World in Cyberspace*, Plenum Trade, New York.

Livingstone, S. (2002), *Young People and New Media: Childhood and the Changing Media Environment*, SAGE, London/Thousand Oaks, CA.

Livingstone, S. and Bober, M. (2004), *UK Children Go Online: Surveying the Experience of Young People and Their Parents*, London: London School of Economics.

Ludvigsen, S., Lund, A. and Säljö, R. (eds) (2007), *Learning in Social Practices: ICT and New Artifacts – Transformation of Social and Cultural Practices*, Pergamon, London.

MacKenzie, D.A. and Wajcman, J. (eds) (1999), *The Social Shaping of Technology*, second edition, Open University Press, Buckingham.

Madden, M. and Fox, S. (2006), *Riding the Waves of 'Web 2.0': More Than a Buzzword, But Still Not Easily Defined*, Pew Internet and American Life Project. Online. Available at: www.pewinternet.org/~/media/Files/Reports/2006/PIP_Web_2.0.pdf.pdf [accessed 27 June 2005].

Marx, K. and Engels, F. (1970), *The German Ideology*, ed. C.J. Arthur, Lawrence & Wishart, London.

McLuhan, M. (1962), *The Gutenberg Galaxy: The Making of Typographic Man*, University of Toronto Press, Toronto.

—— (1994), *Understanding Media: The Extensions of Man*, intro. and ed. by L.H. Lapham, MIT Press, Cambridge, MA/London.

Mcmillan, S.J. and Morrison, M. (2006), 'Coming of Age with the Internet: A Qualitative Exploration of How the Internet Has Become an Integral Part of Young People's Lives', *New Media Society*, 8(1): 73–95.

McRobbie, A. (1975), 'Girls and Subculture', in S. Hall and T. Jefferson (eds), *Resistance through Ritual: Youth Subcultures in Post-War Britain*, Hutchinson, London, pp. 209–222.

Metcalfe, J. and Shimamura, A.P. (1994), *Metacognition: Knowing About Knowing*, MIT Press, Cambridge, MA/London.

Moll, L.C. and Greenberg, J. (1990), 'Creating zones of possibilities: combining social contexts for instruction', in L.C. Moll (ed.), *Vygotsky and Education*, Cambridge University Press, Cambridge.

Moll, L.C., Tapia, J. and Whitmore, K.F. (1997), 'Living Knowledge: The Social Distribution of Cultural Resources for Thinking', in G. Salomon (ed.), *Distributed Cognitions: Psychological and Educational Considerations*, Cambridge University Press, Cambridge, pp. 139–162.

Moll, L.C., Amanti, C., Neff, D. and González, N. (1992), 'Funds of Knowledge for Teaching: Using a Qualitative Approach to Connect Homes and Classrooms', *Theory into Practice*, 31(2): 132–141.

Moran, C. and Hawisher, G. E. (1998), 'Rhetorics and Languages of Electronic Mail', in I. Snyder (ed.), *Page to Screen: Taking Literacy into the Electronic Era*, Routledge, London, pp. 80–101.

Muukkonen, H., Lakkala, M. and Hakkarainen, K. (2005), 'Technology-Mediation and Tutoring: How Do They Shape Progressive Inquiry Discourse?' *Journal of the Learning Sciences*, 4(4): 527–566.

Nardi, B.A., Whittaker, S. and Schwarz, H. (2002), 'NetWORKers and Their Activity in Intensional Networks', *Computer Supported Cooperative Work*, 11(1–2): 205–242.

Nardi, B.A., Schiano, D.J., Gumbrecht, M. and Swartz, L. (2004), 'Why We Blog', *Communications of the ACM*, 47(12): 41–46.

New London Group (1996), 'A Pedagogy of Multiliteracies: Designing Social Futures', *Harvard Educational Review*, 66(1): 60–92.

—— (2000), 'A Pedagogy of Multiliteracies: Designing Social Futures', in B. Cope and M. Kalantzis (eds), *Multiliteracies: Literacy Learning and the Design of Social Futures*, Routledge, London, pp. 9–42.

Norman, D. (1993), *Things That Make Us Smart: Defending Human Attributes in the Age of the Machine*, Addison-Wesley Pub. Co, Reading, MA.

—— (2002), *The Design of Everyday Things*, Basic Books, New York.

Olson, D.R. (1994), *The World on Paper: The Conceptual and Cognitive Implications of Writing and Reading*, Cambridge University Press, Cambridge/New York.

—— (1995), 'Writing and the Mind', in J.V. Wertsch, P. del Río and A. Alvarez (eds), *Sociocultural Studies of Mind*, Cambridge University Press, Cambridge.

O'Reilly, T. (2005), *What Is Web 2.0: Design Patterns and Business Models for the Next Generation of Software*. Online. Available at: http://tim.oreilly.com/pub/a/ oreilly/ tim/news/2005/09/30/what-is-web-20.html?page=1 [accessed 24 August 2009].

Pea, R.D. (1985), 'Beyond Amplification: Using the Computer to Reorganize Mental Functioning', *Educational Psychologist*, 20(4): 167–182.

—— (1997), 'Practices of Distributed Intelligence and Designs for Education', in G. Salomon (ed.), *Distributed Cognitions: Psychological and Educational Considerations*, Cambridge University Press, Cambridge, pp. 47–87.

—— (2004), 'The Social and Technological Dimensions of Scaffolding and Related Theoretical Concepts for Learning, Education, and Human Activity', *Journal of the Learning Sciences*, 13(3): 423–451.

Perkins, D.N. (1997), 'Person-Plus: A Distributed View of Thinking and Learning', in G. Salomon (ed.), *Distributed Cognitions: Psychological and Educational Considerations*, Cambridge University Press, Cambridge, pp. 88–110.

Pool, I. de S. (1983), *Technologies of Freedom*, Belknap Press, Cambridge, MA.

Preece, J., Rogers, Y. and Sharp, H. (2002), *Interaction Design: Beyond Human-Computer Interaction*, Wiley, New York.

Resnick, L.B. (1996), 'Shared Cognition: Thinking as Social Practice', in L.B. Resnick, J.M. Levine and S.D. Teasley (eds), *Perspectives on Socially Shared Cognition*, American Psychological Association, Washington, DC., pp. 1–22.

Rikard, G.L. and Langley, D.J. (1995), 'The Think Aloud Procedure: A Research Technique for Gaining Insight into the Student Perspective', *The Physical Educator*, 52(2): 83–97.

Robson, C. (2002), *Real World Research: A Resource for Social Scientists and Practitioner-Researchers*, second edition, Blackwell, Oxford.

Rogoff, B. (1990), *Apprenticeship in Thinking: Cognitive Development in Social Context*, Oxford University Press, New York/Oxford.

—— (2003), *The Cultural Nature of Human Development*, Oxford University Press, Oxford/New York.

Rogoff, B. and Lave, J. (eds) (1984), *Everyday Cognition: Its Development in Social Context*, Harvard University Press, Cambridge, MA.

Rogoff, B. and Wertsch, J.V. (1984), *Children's Learning in The 'Zone of Proximal Development'*, Jossey-Bass, San Francisco, CA.

Rogoff, B., Chavajay, P., Heath, S.B. and Society for Research in Child Development (1993), *Guided Participation in Cultural Activity by Toddlers and Caregivers*, University of Chicago Press, Chicago, IL.

Rückriem, G. (2009), 'Digital technology and mediation: a challenge to activity theory', in A. Sannino, H. Daniels and K. Gutiérrez (eds), *Learning and Expanding with Activity Theory*, Cambridge University Press, Cambridge.

Säljö, R. (1999), 'Learning as the Use of Tools: A Sociocultural Approach on the Human-Technology Link', in K. Littleton and P. Light (eds), *Learning with Computers: Analysing Productive Interactions*, Routledge, London.

—— (2004), 'Educational Conversations and Information Technological Revolutions in Human History', in L.-E. Axelsson, K. Bodin, T. Persson, R. Sanyang and I. Svensson (eds), *Folkbildning.Net: An Anthology About 'Folkbildning' and Flexible Learning*, second revised edition, Stockholm: The Swedish National Council of Adult Education, pp. 211–227. Online. Available at: www. resurs. folkbildning.net/download/317/ant2eng__content_etc.pdf [accessed 22 July 2006].

Salmon, G. (2002), *E-tivities: The Key to Active Online Learning*, Kogan Page: London.

Schön, D.A. (1983), *The Reflective Practitioner: How Professionals Think in Action*, Basic Books, New York.

—— (1987), *Educating the Reflective Practitioner: Toward a New Design for Teaching and Learning in the Professions*, Jossey-Bass, San Francisco, CA.

Scribner, S. (1988), 'Studying Working Intelligence', in B. Rogoff and J. Lave (eds), *Everyday Cognition: Its Development in Social Contexts*, Cambridge University Press, Cambridge, pp. 9–40.

Scribner, S. and Cole, M. (1981), *The Psychology of Literacy*, Harvard University Press, Cambridge, MA.

Sefton-Green, J. (ed.) (1998), *Digital Diversions: Youth Culture in the Age of Multimedia*, UCL Press, London.

—— (2004), 'The "End of School" or just "Out of School"? ICT, the Home and Digital Cultures', in C. Durrant and C. Beavis (eds), *P(ICT)ures of English: Teachers, Learners and Technology*, Wakefield Press, Kent Town, SA, pp. 162–174.

Selwyn, N., Gorard, S. and Furlong, J. (2006), *Adult Learning in the Digital Age: Information Technology and the Learning Society*, Routledge, London.

Shaffer, D.W. (2005), 'Epistemic Games', *Innovate*, 1(6). Online. Available at: www. innovateonline.info/pdf/vol1_issue6/Epistemic_Games.pdf [accessed 4 December 2005].

Shaffer, D.W. and Resnick, M. (1999), '"Thick" Authenticity: New Media and Authentic Learning', *Journal of Interactive Learning Research*, 10(2): 195–215.

Sharpe, R., Benfield, G., Roberts, G. and Francis, R. (2006), *The Undergraduate Experience of Blended E-Learning: A Review of UK Literature and Practice*, The Higher Educational Academy. Online. Available at: www.heacademy.ac.uk/assets/ York/ documents/ourwork/research/literature_reviews/blended_elearning_exec_ summary_1.pdf [accessed 27 June 2006].

Snyder, I. (ed.) (1998), *Page to Screen: Taking Literacy into the Electronic Era*, Routledge, London.

—— (ed.) (2002), *Silicon Literacies: Communication, Innovation and Education in The Electronic Age*, Routledge, London.

Somekh, B. (2004), 'Taking the Sociological Imagination to School: An Analysis of the (Lack of) Impact of Information and Communication Technologies on Education Systems', *Technology Pedagogy and Education*, 13(2): 163–181.

Stake, R.E. (2000), 'The Case Study Method in Social Inquiry', in M. Hammersley, P. Foster and R. Gomm (eds), *Case Study Method: Key Issues, Key Texts*, SAGE, London, pp. 19–27.

Steinkuehler, C.A. and Williams, D. (2006), 'Where everybody knows your (screen) name: Online games as "third places"', *Journal of Computer-Mediated Communications*, 11(4): article 1.

Street, B.V. (1984), *Literacy in Theory and Practice*, Cambridge University Press, Cambridge.

Tapscott, D. (1998), *Growing up Digital: The Rise of the Net Generation*. McGraw-Hill, New York/London.

Tobin, J. (1998), 'An American *Otaku* (or, a Boy's Virtual Life on the Net)', in J. Sefton-Green (ed.), *Digital Diversions: Youth Culture in the Age of Multimedia*, UCL Press, London, pp. 106–127.

Turkle, S. (1984), *The Second Self: Computers and the Human Spirit*, Granada, London.

—— (1997), *Life on the Screen: Identity in the Age of the Internet*, Phoenix, London.

Tyner, K.R. (1998), *Literacy in a Digital World: Teaching and Learning in the Age of Information*, Erlbaum, Mahwah, NJ.

Valsiner, J. (1997), *Culture and the Development of Children's Action: A Theory of Human Development*, second edition, Wiley, Chichester/New York.

Vygotsky, L.S. (1978), *Mind in Society: The Development of Higher Psychological Processes*, trans. and ed. M. Cole, V. John-Steiner, S. Scribner and E. Souberman, Harvard University Press, Cambridge, MA/London.

—— (ed.), (1986), *Thought and Language*, new translation, MIT Press, Cambridge, MA.

—— (1987), *The Collected Works of L.S. Vygotsky*, ed. R.W. Rieber, Kluwer Academic/Plenum Press, New York/London.

—— (1997), *The Collected Works of L.S. Vygotsky, Vol. 4: The History of the Development of Higher Mental Functions*, Plenum Press, New York/London.

Wartofsky, M.W. (1979), *Models: Representation and the Scientific Understanding*, D. Reidel Pub. Co, Dordrecht/Boston, MA.

Wenger, E. (1998), *Communities of Practice: Learning, Meaning, and Identity*, Cambridge University Press, Cambridge.

Wertsch, J.V. (1985), *Vygotsky and the Social Formation of Mind*, Harvard University Press, Cambridge, MA/London.

—— (1991), *Voices of the Mind: A Sociocultural Approach to Mediated Action*, Harvester Wheatsheaf, London.

—— (1998), *Mind as Action*, Oxford University Press, New York/Oxford.

—— (2002), *Voices of Collective Remembering*, Cambridge University Press, Cambridge.

Wertsch, J.V., del Río, P. and Alvarez, A. (1995), 'History, Action and Mediation', in J.V. Wertsch, P. del Río and A. Alvarez (eds), *Sociocultural Studies of Mind*, Cambridge University Press, Cambridge, pp. 1–37.

White, D. (2007), *Spire Project – Results and Analysis of Web 2.0 Services Survey*, Joint Information Systems Committee, Oxford. Online. Available at: www.jisc.ac.uk/media/documents/programmes/digitalrepositories/spiresurvey.pdf [accessed 25 July 2007].

Williams, R. (1961), *The Long Revolution*, Chatto & Windus, London.

—— (1983), *Culture and Society, 1780–1950*, Columbia University Press, New York.

—— (2003), *Television: Technology and Cultural Form*, Routledge, London.

Willis, P. (1978), *Learning to Labour: How Working Class Kids Get Working Class Jobs*, Saxon House, Farnborough.

—— (2005), 'Culture, Institution, Differentiation', in K. Gelder (ed.), *The Subcultures Reader*, second edition, Routledge, London/New York.

Wundt, W. (1921), *Elements of Folk Psychology*, Allen & Unwin, London.

Wood, D., Bruner, J. and Ross, G. (1976), 'The Role of Tutoring in Problem Solving', *Journal of Child Psychology*, 17(2): 89–100.

Young, J. (2005), 'The Subterranean World of Play', in K. Gelder (ed.), *The Subcultures Reader*, second edition, Routledge, London/New York.

Zinchenko, V.P. (1985), 'Vygotsky's Ideas About Units of Analysis for the Mind', in J.V. Wertsch (ed.), *Culture, Communication, and Cognition: Vygotskian Perspectives*, Cambridge University Press, Cambridge, pp. 94–118.

Index

Note: Page numbers in *italic* denote tables. Those in **bold** denote figures.

2001: A Space Odyssey 56

Abbot, C. 38
activity theorists 28–9
ad-busting 11
adoption choices 73–4
Adorno, T.W. 8–9
Adult Learning in the Digital Age 15
agency: and mediation 26–7
'An American *Otaku*' 1
anxiety of choice: information resources 72
AOL 89
appropriation, creative *see* creative appropriation
Arcanium (video game) 35
attention economics: and cyberspace 72–3

Bakhtin, Mikhail 23, 57–8
Bateson, Gregory 23, 31, 34
Bergson, H. 56
Birmingham School of Cultural Studies 11
Blustein, H. 17
Bober, M. 13
breaking away 32, 33, 34, 58–61, 118
Bruner, Jerome 94, 95
Burke, Kenneth 23

Capital 29
case studies: 'An American *Otaku*' 1; students' use of new media 18–21;

Why Heather Can Write 1–2 *see also* vignettes
Castells, M. 112
Cazden, Courtney 136*n*2.2
challenges and choices: learner as designer 50–1; new media literacies 71–4, 89–92; and opportunities of media converge 116–17
child development: research 27
Churchill, Winston 2
Clark, Andy 43
Coffield, F. 16
cognitive anthropology 31–2
cognitive ecology design: vignette 46–7
cognitive labour: division of 47, 117–18
cognitive science 23
Cole, Michael 23–4, 28, 29, 40, 56
collaborative online learning: beyond university 77–8; research into 75–6
college students: construction of 16–17; demographics *19*; in study 18–19
commitment, internalized 73
committed learning 104
communities of practice model 32, 34
Computer Supported Collaborative Learning (CSCL) 75
conceptual development 122
convergence culture 11
Convergence Culture: Where Old and New Media Collide 11, 120
Cope, Bill 136*n*2.2
creative appropriation: and authentic need 64–6; concept of 57–8; and

cultural change 66–7; future research 124–5; and projective identity 68–71; vignettes 59–71
Crook, C. 8, 17, 75
CSCL (Computer Supported Collaborative Learning) *see* Computer Supported Collaborative Learning
cultural anthropology 31
cultural change: creative appropriation and 66–7
cultural-historical development 24
The Cultural Practice of Study 17
'cultural psychology' 136*n*1
cultural tools: mediation through 24–6
culture industry 8–12
cyber-economics 23
cyborgification 43

D'Arcy, C. 31, 77
data collection 20–1, 29, 130–4
de Certeau, M. 56, 58
decentring metaphor 118–19
Dennett, Daniel 43
dependency management 92
deployment 43–4
Derry, J. 56
design states 52–4
design work: design objectives 51; designing alone 50–1; importance of 44; scope of 48–9
development research agenda 128–9
Developmental Work Research (DWR) *see* DWR
digital literacies 37
digital media literacy theories 23
digital tools: mediation through 24–6
digitally mediated practice: as new media literacy 37–40
double bind situations 34, 59–61, 87
double stimulation method 26
DWR (Developmental Work Research) 128–9

e-mail correspondence: data collection 133
eBay 39
(self)education: future of 15, 16–18
educational policy: implications for 121–3

educational practice: implications for 121–3
Edwards, A. 31, 77–8
electronic seminars 75
emotive designs 54–5
enabling constraints 17, 51, 68, 92, 116
Encarta 12
Engeström, Yrjö 23, 31, 32–3, 45–6, 114–15
Enzensberger, H.M. 9–10
epistemic games 98
Everquest 97
evolved designs 52–3, 123
expansive learning 31, 32–5
extended mediation triangle 114–16

Facebook 12, 16, 18, 85, 89–90, 120
Facer, K. 13
Fairclough, Norman 136*n*2.2
Fans, Bloggers and Gamers: Exploring Participatory Culture 11
figured worlds 36–7
file-sharing communities 11–12, 120, 125
Flickr 12
'folk' cultures 11
follow-up interviews: data collection 133
Fox, S. 12
Frankfurt School theorists 9
Freire, P. 9
friendship driven practices 15–16
Friendster 12, 84
'funds of living knowledge': concept of 77; cultivating 81–5; formation 78–81; future research 125–6; globally distributed 85–8, 117; nurturing 88–9

game theory 23
game worlds 35
gaming culture 97
Gee, James 35, 40, 95, 97–8, 136*n*2.2
geeking out 16, 99, 127
gender bending 96
genetic method: Vygotsky's 24
Giddens, A. 32
Goldhaber, M. 72
Goodman, Nelson 95

Google 89
guided participation 34

Hall, S. 11
Hine, C. 133
history in laptop 103–4, 107–9
hobbies: involving use of Internet 20
Holland, Dorothy 31, 35, 36, 37, 94, 95, 98–9, 102, 104–5
horizontal development 33, 34
Horkheimer, M. 8
Hutchins, Edwin 31
hybrid ecologies 119

identity: and agency 95–6; and media landscape 13; as mediator 34–5, 67–71; as motivator 34–5, 67–71; and worldmaking 98–102
Identity and Agency in Cultural Worlds 35
Ilyenkov, E.V. 33
immersive game worlds 35
in-depth interviews: data collection 132–3
informal conversations: data collection 130
information resources: Internet 57; quality of 72
inherited designs 52, 123
intent participation 77
interest driven practices 15–16
interests: involving use of Internet 13, 20
interviews: data collection 130–3
Ito, M. 15, 16, 127

Jefferson, T. 11
Jenkins, Henry 1–2, 11, 12, 39, 102, 112–13, 114, 120
Jochems, W. 76
Jones, S. 17
Joyce, M. 38

Kalantzis, Mary 136n2.2
Kazaar 11–12
Kirschner, P.A. 76
Knobel, Michele 38, 121
'knowing how to know who' 90–1
Kreijns, K. 76

Kress, Gunter 37–8, 44–5, 136n2.2

language: as cultural tool 27
Lankshear, Colin 38, 121
Lave, J. 32
learner as designer: challenges and choices 50–1; future research 123–4; understanding 43–8
learning: Bateson's three types 34; committed 104; media change and 12–16; in zone of proximal development 29–40
Learning to Labour: How Working Class Kids Get Working Class Jobs 9
Lenhart, A. 57
Leont'ev, Alexei 22, 115
Lévy, P. 75, 93
Life on the Screen: Identity in the Age of the Internet 96
lifelong learning agenda 106–10
Light, P. 8, 17, 75
LinkedIn 91
LiveLeak.com 120
Living and Learning with New Media 15
Livingstone, S. 13
locus of agency: for managing learning 8, 63, 112, 117
Luke, Allan 136n2.2
Luke, Carmen 136n2.2
Luria, Alexandre 22

McLuhan, Marshal 66, 112
Mcmillan, S.J. 17
Madden, M. 12
Marx, Karl 29
mass media 9
massively multiplayer online role playing games (MMORPGs) *see* MMORPGs
mature concepts 136n4.1
media change: challenges and choices 72; implications 112–14; and learning 12–16; understanding 8–12
media use, by students: case study 18–21 *see also* vignettes
mediation: concept of 25; through use of cultural tools 24–6
method of double stimulation 26
methodology: data collection 29

Michels, Sarah 136*n*2.2
microblogging 25
microgenesis 24, 29, 38
microsociology 32
Mind in Society 29
mindful design 52, 53–4, 123–4
mindfulness 54, 55
mirror method 128
MMORPGs (massively multiplayer online role playing games) 97
Moll, L.C. 77, 88
Morrison, M. 17
motivation 1–2, 13; and identity 34–5
MSN Messenger 13, 18, 89, 119
MUDs (Multi-User Dungeons) 96–7
multimodality theory 23, 44–5
Muukkonen, H. 75–6
My Space 12, 15–16

'N-Geners' 13
Nakata, Martin 136*n*2.2
Napster 11–12, 17, 120
Nardi, B.A. 76
National Grid for Learning 39
Natural-Born Cyborgs 43
networks: personal 84; use of 75–6
new literacy movement 23
New London Group 40, 44
new media literacies: challenges 71–4, 89–92
new media literacy theories 23, 37–40
Norman, D. 42

object-motives 28–9, 102
object-orientated activities: study of 28–9
observation notes: data collection 131
offloading 43
Olson, D.R. 40, 122
online discussion forums 75–6
online encyclopaedia 12
ontogeny 24
ontological innovation 122
opportunities: and challenges of media converge 116–17

Page to Screen: Taking Literacy into the Electronic Era 38
participatory culture 11–12, 134

Perkins, D.N. 30, 118
personalized learning environments 4
play 13, 102–3, 126–7
Pool, I. de S. 10
The Practice of Everyday Life 58
pre-interview questionnaires: data collection 131
projective identities 35–7, 68–71, 85, 100, 102, 103, 107, 115–16, 127
psycho-social moratoriums: virtual figured worlds as 96–7
The Psychology of Literacy 40

quasi-virtual ecologies 2–3

reductive analysis 28
relational agency 31, 77–8, 80, 90, 91–2
research: child development 27; further 123–8
Resistance through Rituals 11
retrospective virtual ethnography: data collection 20, 133–4
The rhetorics and Languages of Electronic Mail 38
The Rise of the Net Generation 12–13
The Rise of the Networked Society 112
Rogoff, Barbara 31, 77
Roller Coaster Tycoon 98
Roman Catholicism 36

Säljö, R. 75, 92–3
scaffolding 30, 77, 116–17
Scribner, S. 29, 40
Second Life 13, 97
self-authoring spaces: virtually figured worlds as 104–6
self-directed learning activity: culture of 4
self education: future of 15, 16–18
self-making: higher university 115–16; narrative construction 95–7; virtual figured worlds 98–102; virtual role-play 96–7
self-motivated learning 97
Selwyn, N. 15
serious play 102–3, 126–7
Shaffer, David 98
Sharpe, R. 18

silicon literacies 37
Silicon Literacies: Communication, Innovation and Education in the Electronic Age 38
SimCity 2000 98
'site of struggle': culture as 11
Skype 12, 13, 18, 89, 120
Snyder, Illana 38
social networking sites 12, 16, 18, 84–5, 89, 90–1
Social Shaping of Technology 66
sociocultural and activity theory: and case study 20; overview 22–31
sociocultural theory 66
Soviet school of cultural-historical psychology 22–3, 28, 66
speech: as tool of tools 27
Stake, R.E. 122
Steinkuehler, C.A. 97
stimulated response: data collection 131–2
structuration theory 32
students *see* college students
studies: students' use of new media 18–21
study groups vignette 79–80
subject-tool-object triangle 114–15

Tapscott, D. 12–13
techno literacies 37
techno media literacy theories 23
technological determinism 66
Technologies of Freedom 10
TED (Technology, Entertainment and Design) talks 119–20
Textual Poachers: Television Fans and Participatory Culture 11
Things That Make Us Smart 42
Thought and Language 23
Tobin, J. 1
tool-mediated actions: as unit of analysis 28–9
tools: mediation through 24–6
Turkle, Sherry 95, 96
Twitter 25

UK *Children Go Online* 13
unit of analysis 28–9

video game (Arcanium) 35
vignettes: adoption choices 73; breaking away 59–61; creative appropriation 59–63; design of cognitive ecology 46–7; double bind situations 59–61; and funds of living knowledge 78–87; against the grain practices 62–3, 64; lifelong learning agenda 106–10; MSN Messenger 81–3; and projective identity 68, 69, 70–1; study groups 79–80; tactical redeployments 65; virtual filing cabinet design 49; virtually figured worlds 99–100, 101
virtual filing cabinet design: vignette 49
virtually figured worlds: future research 126–7; learning through 97–8; and projective identity 35–7; as psycho-social moratoriums 96–7; as self-making 98–102; as spaces of self-authoring 2–3, 104–6; vignettes 99–100, 101
Vygotsky, Lev 22–3, 25, 26–7, 28, 30, 32, 45, 102, 103, 136*n*4.1
Vygotsky's genetic method 24, 31
Vygotsky's subject-tool-object triangle 114

Warhammer game 1, 37
We are Technology and It is Us 56
Web 2.0 technologies 12, 14, 134
Wenger, E. 32
Wertsch, Jim 22, 23, 25, 66–7, 116, 119
Why Heather Can Write 1–2
Wikipedia 12, 13, 18, 119
Williams, D. 97
Williams, Raymond 11
Willis, P. 9
The Wired World of Second Language Acquisition 38
World of Warcraft 97
Wundt, Wilheim 136*n*2.1

Yahoo 17, 89
YouTube 13, 18, 120

zone of proximal development (ZPD) 78, 102; and learning 29–40